To ~~xxxxx~~ *Best Wishes !*

Honeysucker:

High Country Humor as Odd as an Okra Sandwich

Stephen V. Sprinkle

[signature: Stephen V. Sprinkle]

Ariel sings

"Where the bee sucks, there suck I: In a cowslip's bell I lie;
There I couch when owls do cry. On the bat's back I do fly
After summer merrily.

Merrily, merrily shall I live now
Under the blossom that hangs on the bough."

from **Tempest, Act V, Scene I**
[Where the bee sucks, there suck I]

~ William Shakespeare

This book is a combination of facts and recollections about Stephen Sprinkle's life and certain embellishments. Some names, dates, places, events, and details have been changed, invented, and altered for literary effect. The reader should not consider this book anything other than a work of literature.

Library of Congress Cataloguing-in-Publication Data
Sprinkle, Stephen V.

Honeysucker:

High country humor as odd as an okra sandwich
by Stephen V. Sprinkle – First edition.

ISBN: 978-0-9903672-0-8

Library of Congress Control Number: 2014908474

Dedication

To the finest parents a Honeysucker could ever have,
Hazel Annie Martin Sprinkle & Thedford Guy Sprinkle;
and to my grandparents: on the maternal side,
Bessie Venable Martin & Thomas Hamlin Martin;
and on the paternal side,
Ila Wood Sprinkle & Banister Franklin Sprinkle

They taught me how to mix strength and gentleness,
and they never rained on my dreams.

Honeysucker

Table of Contents

Introduction,
or How to Fix a
Seductive Okra Sandwich

A good story ought to grab your attention like an okra sandwich. Okra, for those who don't know, is a Southern delicacy. It comes from a big plant imported from Africa in the 1700s. The edible bits are the long, green pods, usually covered in fuzzy little transparent whiskers when fresh picked. Never mind. You can brush the hairs right off. Some call okra pods "Lady Fingers"—but I never saw any lady with fingers like that, unless she was infected with a terrible case of bright green jealousy. But, I digress . . .

What makes okra such a provocative ingredient for a sandwich is trying to figure out how to eat it, and what the taste reminds you of when you do. Okra pickles like a champ. It surely stews up nicely—boiled just right, it's slicker than a gob of Crisco on your bald headed granddaddy's scalp—the one vegetable you don't have to bother swallowing 'cause it slides down the hatch on its own. Fries up perfectly, too, when

1

dipped in cornmeal and buttermilk, and then plopped in hot grease. Tastes just like fried oysters, fixed that-a-way. Why, you can even candy it. But raw, slapped between two pieces of lite bread ("store-bought bread" for the Yankees in the audience)? Like trying to pull a mad badger out of its hole, the secret to eating such an interesting sandwich is all in how you approach it.

The stories in this collection are odd like that. You need to know how to approach them, too. They come out of experiences from the first eighteen years of my life in the Mountain South, specifically the Scotch-Irish county along the eastern slope of the Blue Ridge Mountains of North Carolina. Like an okra sandwich, even if you don't understand everything about these stories—the religion, for example, or the dialect—you can still enjoy them. I had fun growing up, largely because I inherited a quirky way of looking at the world around me. Wonderfully strange characters populated my childhood. By heritage, culture and imagination, I also have the gift of gab enough to tell the wondrous strangeness of what I see in stories. The history of the Appalachian Mountains is riddled with superb storytellers, like my maternal Great Grandmother, Aradella Hamlin Martin, as you will presently see. Many of the characters in these stories are inspired by my relatives, or actual people I have known. A few are still alive and kicking, though they may not recognize themselves much in the tales I tell. I make no claims to accuracy about anything. As a matter of fact, sitting loose toward actuality is one of the over-arching characteristics of Southern Highland storytelling. One should never water down the sweet oil of anecdote with the vinegar of fact! Hollywood dramatizes its scripts. Why shouldn't a Hillbilly like me?

So, Gentle Reader, forgive errors in fact, or judgment on my part. The humor here is meant to be lighthearted. I hope you receive it in the same spirit as I offer it. Like President Nixon, I accept all the responsibility, and none of the blame. Aspects of the lives and deeds of actual persons, living or dead, have been liberally fictionalized when it seemed funny to do so; and names have been changed here and there to protect the innocent (or the guilty, as the case may be). I owe a great debt of gratitude to my cousin, Jane McCoy, to my splendid administrative assistant at Brite Divinity School, Sandy Brandon, to my photographer, Stephen Feryus, to my graphic designer, Charles Owen, and to my incomparable illustrators, Charlie Rose and Daniel W. Peeler of Peeler-Rose Designs.

The true interest conveyed by these funny, strange, sometimes sad, often ribald stories, is that they boldly take a big bittersweet bite out of the human condition—like Adam and Eve masticating (Ooooh! Big word!) an apple. Occasionally, the mouthfuls of life we chew on, as the Good Book says, are sweet in the mouth, but bitter in the belly. These yarns deal with pain, sorrow, death, and inestimable loss, as well as hilarity and the everyday comedy of our lives. What I have attempted to do with my stories here, then, is akin to slathering a raw okra sandwich with a big dollop of sourwood honey. That's something only a Honeysucker would do, 'cause a Honeysucker knows how to make the most out of a little—to live sweet and large, and suck the marrow out of the Good Life, even from a dry, old husk! Honey on an okra sandwich? That may be a culinary heresy, even a gastronomical outrage—but, like the stories in this book, *it shore is sweet, ain't it!*

~ **Stephen V. Sprinkle**
May Day 2014

Invasion of the Tourists

Where I grew up, there were two small churches and two country stores, and the stores had more members than both churches put together. My neck of the woods was the Foothills of the Blue Ridge Mountains, near one of the most ravishingly beautiful valleys on the Eastern Seaboard. Only ten miles from my childhood home lies Devotion, lush, green, rolling, and as pastoral as a Swiss alpine postal card. A pristine mountain river cut the valley out of the stone of the mountains eons ago, and now Mitchell's River winds like a silver ribbon right down the middle of green hillside pastures, past herds of beef cattle, the slopes of the chinquapin covered hills rife with white-tailed deer that come down to the water to drink at night. Devotion is a spot so rare and inviting that two great robber baron families established hunting lodges and retreats in the coves of the hills back in my Grandmother's day: the R.J. Reynolds tobacco-fortune family, and the Hanes textile-empire family. These grandees preserved whole ranges of the great blue mountains for themselves, building dog kennels, wild turkey coops, and even grading off a small airstrip to accommodate private aircraft—all now lying disused, silent, and mostly abandoned by later generations of the rich whose summer diversions tend toward the Caribbean or the Riviera rather than a cool, Blue Ridge Mountain hideaway. Their loss! Give me Devotion any day.

Tourists from up North eventually discovered the charms of Devotion and the peculiarity of mountain folk, and whopper tour buses infested with sun-spectacled, portly, camera-wielding seniors, bedecked in mismatched pastels and god-awful plaids, began chugging up and down the narrow roads of home, searching for a cold soda pop and directions to Devotion. Cousin Gladys's Country Store was a sure stop.

Uncle Zeke,
the Sphinx of Salem Fork

Cousin Gladys was skinny as a rail and weathered by hard work, with big, sparkly cat's eye glasses perched on her nose. She owned and operated her two-gas pump, cinder block store for decades, the only store on the Zephyr Road to the valley. Gladys was what we called a "straight razor-toed bid'ness woman," no fool when it came to making a living—the equal of any man around. She stocked a little of everything in that little store: wonders like real sugar candy canes, county hams hanging from the rafters, great orange wheels of cheddar cheese, citrus, bananas, seasonal fruits and vegetables in wooden bins, sourwood honey (honeycomb in the jar, of course), new crop molasses, and ice cold drinks tempting customers to fill up their pickup trucks with brown paper sacks full of the stuff. Men from all around gathered at Gladys's Store to talk politics, brag big on raccoon hunts, and relax before going back to work their fields. Gladys's was the social hub of the community, drawing folks up from the foothills, and families come down from the mountains to buy what they couldn't grow—and share the latest gossip.

For tourists seeking a hillbilly encounter with the local life forms, then, Gladys's Store was a sure fire destination. Herds and gaggles of them descended on the store, providing a windfall for Gladys who rang her cash register like a church bell day and night.

Photos taken with "gen-u-whine" mountain folk were trophies for the tourists, who annoyed the daylights out of the more picturesque of Gladys's regulars with pleas to "stand still," and "look this way," when some old mountaineer left the store and strode through the gawkers, making a break for home. But Uncle Zeke couldn't move that fast due to his age, and for that matter usually didn't try to get away from them anyway.

Uncle Zeke could normally be found sitting in one of Gladys's ladder backed chairs just outside the entrance to the store. He was the real deal: ancient, even by old folks' standards, habitually decked out in a careworn, old white shirt and bibbed denim overalls, shod with a pair of brogans, and topped off with a broad brimmed felt hat you might recognize from a vintage Hatfields and McCoys photo. Thin as a toothpick, with a set of bushy, white eyebrows and a white moustache so long and thick that it covered his lips completely and muffled his speech, he sat up straight as an iron fire poker in that chair every morning and afternoon of the world, speaking fewer words than any man I ever knew. There was nothing wrong with Uncle Zeke's mind despite his age, though. Naw, sir! His steel gray eyes, peering out from underneath the brim of his hat, never missed a thing.

One hot afternoon in the late 1960s, a tourist disgorged from a bus with Ohio license plates beset Uncle Zeke with a new fangled contraption few people around home had ever seen—a portable tape recorder, the reel-to-reel kind before cassettes, one that needed a plug-in microphone in order to record anything. As the tour paparazzi encircled Uncle Zeke sitting in his chair, calling him by name to "look here!" and "smile!" (How would anybody know if he did?), the guy with the recorder thrust his microphone up under his nose and insisted,

"Hey, you, say something to me!"

No reply.

"Say something, buddy! Say something!"

Stonier silence . . .

"Sir! Sir! Have you lived here all your life?"

The old man yawned: "Naw. Not yet . . . !"

"The Devil flew into 'em!"

The closest country store to Devotion belonged to the Grayback boys, two brothers who operated a store they inherited from their old man. Grayback's Store sat at the crossroads just before descending into the valley, the last stop where you could get yourself a pack of four-cornered nabs, a pack of peanuts, a cold R.C. Cola (Royal Crown, that is), and answer the call of nature before driving further.

To the untrained eye, the Grayback boys seemed just as quaint and rustic as Uncle Zeke, and the store, though clean as a new washed baby's bum, was clearly more primitive than Cousin Gladys's. For one thing, there were no indoor facilities. Instead, the boys had built a wooden back-to-back outdoor toilet by the side of the road, a four-holer, with a Men's entrance to the left, a Women's entrance to the right, and a common wall between them. Skeptics about relieving themselves in a "Johnny house" were welcome to forego the comforts of the country, and just keep crossing their legs evermore tightly. Urgency overcame most of these misgivings rather readily.

A Johnny house is a marvel of hillbilly sanitary technology. The wooden superstructure, the "house," rests over a four-to-six foot deep pit dug out to accommodate the excreta. It was air conditioned in the wintertime. For modesty's sake, there were no windows. At most, a quarter moon cutout was provided in the door to admit a little light. Users entered the proper side to view a "commodious" room with a box bench built against the interior wall, covered by a smoothly planed shelf of planks into which two oval holes were neatly cut, side-by-side with no partition in between. This facilitated conversation, a Southern art form.

Sanitary supplies consisted of a Sears or J.C. Penney catalogue hanging by a wire within easy grasp of each user. One simply tore a sheet or two from the catalogue, and rubbed them vigorously between one's hands until the paper grew soft and pliable enough to use. In the absence of these sanitary reading materials, there might be two buckets of corncobs, one with red cobs (referring to the color of the cob after the kernels had been shelled), and the other with white ones. Herein lies the custom and science of the colors: a user chose a red cob or two to start the sanitary process, and then used a white cob as a test stick to see if another red one was needed—ingenious, no?

In the summertime, yellow jackets, bees, and wasps of several species frequented the pit doing God knows what down there, so it was best to settle one's business pretty quickly and be on one's way, rather than risk stirring up the swarm below. Contrary to intuition, there was little or no aroma of nature in a well-maintained Johnny house, such as the Grayback boys provided the public. A pail of powdered lime with a scoop sat next to the cob buckets. When finished, it was understood by all the initiated that the last act before departing was to dump a generous scoop of lime down the hole, the hillbilly alternative to flushing the bowl.

Travelers who thought the Grayback boys were stupid, and made little secret of it in the store, could have a surprise when they asked for the facilities. Old folks used to say that, once a rude person stirred the Graybacks up, "The Devil flew in 'em." You see, the boys had taken advantage of Surry Community College up the road in Dobson, and trained in electronics. After waiting for the unsuspecting target to get into the outhouse (especially arrogant, fussy old tourists, their favorite marks), with ample time to nestle onto the seat like a snowbird on its nest, the boys switched on a speaker they had planted beneath the seat. An underground cord ran from the hidden speaker into the back office of the store, where the boys had rigged up a high fidelity microphone. All they had to do was flip the switch.

The target, caught in a gastric *flagrante delicto*, heard a rich, baritone voice rising up unexpectedly from below:

"Excooze me, Ma'am! Would you mind scootin' over to the other side? Me and my brother are a-tryin' to paint down here!"

Like being shot out of a gun, here she would come, bursting out the door without a backward glance, tangled up with a pair of pantyhose around the ankles! My Gawd, what a moon dance!

White Liquor

Before marijuana there was white liquor. Name it what you will—moonshine, bootleg whiskey, rotgut, hooch, white lightning, ol' pop skull, or the-hair-of-the-dog-that-bit-you—the illegal manufacture of non-tax paid, distilled alcohol is as deeply ingrained in the culture of the Mountain South as stock car racing and cropping tobacco. As a source of supplemental income, when everything else failed, moonshining got many a mountain family through cold winters with food on the table. But the art of making the liquor and dodging the law goes 'way beyond economics. Moonshining is a combination of legacy and legend. It's a matter of Hillbilly, Scotch-Irish Pride.

Ol' Man Leemie made the stuff for the better part of his eighty-seven years on this planet and extolled its virtues with the enthusiasm of an evangelist: "White liquor!" he liked to say. "It freshens the breath, whitens the teeth, and makes childbirth a pleasure!" Pine splinter-skinny and just as sharp, Ol' Man Leemie was a sight in his faded bibbed overalls, the kind with the "Red Camel" label on the chest, a non-descript flannel shirt, his dusty gray fedora sweated through around the crown, and a fist-sized chaw of plug tobacco perpetually pooching his cheek out. He walked with a stoop, and talked with a high-pitched, nasal twang common to men born on the mountainside. But Mr. Leemie was no hayseed. Naw, sir! He was a genius, a genu-whine moonshine innovator.

Now, revenuers who scoured the hills and hollows searching out liquor stills to bust up and moonshiners to arrest had a built-in advantage, since their quarry habitually worked their stills in the usual hidey holes: dense stands of forest pines, sheltered ravines (called "hollers"), and behind nearly impenetrable slicks of mountain laurel. No matter how well concealed a liquor still might be, sooner or later, anything that just sits in one place can finally be found. But Leemie made moonshining portable: he built a rocket still on the platform of a tobacco slide—a narrow, sturdy, wooden sled used in the harvesting or "priming" of tobacco—and hitched it to a good mule. He was the Phantom of the white liquor world. He never made more than a single batch in any given place, then pulled the still to one site after another with maddening frequency for generations of revenuers he eluded.

Ol' Man Leemie even invented curbside service! Before entertainment branched out to drive-in theatres and supper clubs in Mount Airy, Elkin, and Pilot Mountain, locals would hold dances in each other's homes, called "cotillions." The men would move the furniture out of the large, high ceilinged rooms, and the women would spread corn meal on the hardwood floors so that the dancers would have no trouble slipping and sliding their shoes to the ballads and breakdowns played by the string bands who'd strum, pick, and grin at the drop of a hat (and for the occasional complimentary Mason jar of white lightning). The night air rang with the sounds of banjos, guitars, and the scratchy, high-pitched whine of fiddles. While the women laid out food in the kitchen, the men stepped out back with empty jars to partake of the freshest moonshine in Surry County, conveniently delivered to the doorstep, courtesy of Ol' Man Leemie and his mule, Black Beck. After he sold out, Mr. Leemie would break down the still, pack it back onto the tobacco slide, and disappear into the dark from whence he came, clucking and murmuring to his old mule, "Ho, Beck! Giddyap! G-e-e-e! Gee, now!"

Long after other bootleggers had been put out of commission, Ol' Man Leemie was still going strong. The revenuers who eventually caught him claimed they had outfoxed the old man. No way. What did him in was a mixture of betrayal and dumb luck. Money started being spread around to loosen up some tongues. It worked.

One of Mr. Leemie's distant cousins tipped off the Federals, suggesting a favorite mule path of his, and the agents set an ambush. As Ol' Man Leemie drove Black Beck through a grove of particularly large forest pines, the bushwhackers hid behind the trees. All of a sudden, the boss man stepped out of hiding and shouted, "Federal Agents! You're under arrest!"

Mr. Leemie was well past eighty, but he could run like a scalded-assed ape! He left the boss man grabbing at empty air, and outran five agents, even clearing a two-foot rock wall that jutted up from the forest floor . . . but one of those "damned revenuers" hid behind the tree the old man had to run past. All the agent had to do was step out of the shadows and wrap his arms around Mr. Leemie.

Nobody felt good about locking up such an old timer in a jail cell. Even the magistrate paid him the supreme compliment, calling him a "mountain legend" as he passed sentence. Leemie lived a few more years after he got out. Some say he built his last liquor still underneath a hog pen! What gave him away that time was his thriftiness. Instead of burying the cooked off corn mash like he probably should have, Ol' Man Leemie couldn't bear to waste it. So, he fed it to the hogs. The hogs got so drunk from it, I guess that even a damn dumb revenuer couldn't help noticing!

Living on Borrowed Time

Since I was four years old, I have lived rather happily on borrowed time. At our house, we had central oil heat, provided by a noisy clatter trap of a furnace that dispensed warmth through metal registers in the baseboards at floor level. This detail sets the stage for my earliest remembered encounter with my mortality, since my first dog, Jim, loved to rest right in front of the living room register, soaking up the heat as he lay belly-down on the grey linoleum tile, frog-style, with his hind feet straight out behind him.

Jim, the Boston Terrier, was my first, most beloved childhood pet. At one time or another, I had been allowed to have 18 rabbits (three of them albinos with rosy-red eyes, like binge drunkards); three Rhode Island Red hens, named for my mother's sisters (much to their chagrin); a school of short-lived neon tetras (fish, for the uninitiated); and a chameleon, most properly classified as an anole, named Clem, for Clem Kaddiddlehopper. But there was only one Jim.

17

For the Christmas of my third year, my Uncle Woodrow, standing in as a reasonable facsimile of Santa Claus, delivered the most adorable little black and white, just-weaned Boston Terrier puppy to me, festooned with a big red bow for a collar. He was all eyes peering out from his smooshed-in face: jet black surrounding his orbits and extending up to a set of perky ears, separated by a bold, white blaze that streaked up his considerable forehead. As I took him in my arms, squealing with delight ("Thank you, thank you, Uncle Wood!"), my new puppy licked me on the nose—and it was bonded love between us from that moment onward for the next 18 years of our lives.

Since Mama was my chief consultant in all things, I set straightaway to the serious work of choosing a name for my new puppy, with her acting as sage and advisor. Dad didn't have anything to say in the matter, but he didn't seem to lose sleep over it—he was snoring, as usual, in his enormous leather armchair, tuckered out from building my toys all night for Christmas morning.

Those droll, usual names for dogs in our community—Spike, Fido, Blackie, Mutt—struck me as simply too pedestrian. "I'll name him 'James,'" I said.

"That's a little too formal, don't you think?" Mama said. "Think of how you'll sound calling him 'James! James!' out the back door at suppertime."

"Then, how about 'Jim Dog'?"

"Better," Mama said. "Shorter names are easier to call, though." "Okay, then, how 'bout 'Jim'? Just 'Jim'?"

"Perfect," she said. And it was settled! "Jim" it was!

Dad was usually away doing business on the tobacco market, so the three of us remaining, Mama, Jim, and I, held down the fort while he was gone. On one of his return trips, Dad brought me a peashooter, a mischief-maker toy Mama had misgivings about from the start. But Dad's admonitions to her, "Aw, let him be a boy, Hazel," won out, and I had great fun with it, mostly at poor Jim's expense.

You see, Jim was slender, not beefy like his English bulldog ancestors, so the cool Spring breezes made him shiver. When Mama ran the furnace, luscious warm air surged from the floor registers in the baseboards of the walls, and heated the linoleum toasty—tailor made for a chilly, little Boston bull. Jim's favorite heat register was in the wall of the living room, the one separating it from the kitchen where Mama was cooking up fish sticks and French fries for my supper just before "The Mickey Mouse Club" came on our black-and-white RCA Victor television (I will forever associate "The Mickey Mouse Club" with the flavor of frozen fish sticks and crinkle cut French fries). Jim would settle down right in front of that heat register, snoozing away, while Mama clattered away in the kitchen—and I crept around the couch to surprise my little canine with my peashooter, yet again.

With a little practice, I had become proficient with the peashooter, which was nothing more than a length of candy-striped plastic drinking straw, with a large enough bore to accommodate a little dried pea. Yep. That was all I had for ammunition—a pocket full of dried field peas; but in my hands, they were mighty enough to irritate the daylights out of a snoozing Boston Terrier who never seemed to tire of the game. I had turned my one shot peashooter into a semi-automatic by a deft combination of using my cheeks as magazines for several peas at a time, and my tongue as a swift action loader. I could spring around the corner of the old gray couch, surprise somnolent Jim, and get off three or four rounds onto his rump before he could scramble away 'round the corner to Mama in the kitchen. Jim had drag queen nails both fore and aft, so his frantic attempts to escape my ambushes made him skitter in place for a stroke or two before gaining enough traction to get away.

After the second time I ambushed him in front of the living room heat register that day, Mama had enough. Wow! She was so big, standing there above me with my little plastic peashooter behind my back—wrapped in her apron, wielding a wooden cooking spoon that she pointed right at me.

"You're going to aggravate that dog to death! You need to stop it," she said, accentuating her little sermon with jabs of the spoon. "One day, you're going to swallow one of those peas, and you'll DIE!" she said. Then turning on her heel, she went back to work in the kitchen getting the French fries ready.

"Ha! What's that to me?" I thought, as I went back into hiding for one more good Boston bull ambush before supper. Picking my spot to lie in wait, I checked my supply of dried peas. I put a half-a-handful into the hollow of my right cheek, and went to ground, awaiting Jim to succumb to the lovely warmth of the nicely baked linoleum in front of the heat register.

Here he came, sniffing the air for me, eyes big as saucers, inching toward his favorite spot on the floor. So predictable! With a little grunt, Jim settled down on his stomach, thrusting his white-socked feet out behind, gradually easing down into LaLa Land for his nap, once again.

My tongue worked like a Frenchman on snails, slick and accurate, loading the peashooter for three full times as I sprang around the corner from my hiding place! Three hits on Jim's rump in less than three seconds—a new world's record!—as his little toenails got no purchase on the waxed floor! Then, WHUMP! He lost his balance in his scramble to get away, and belly-flopped before my eyes like something out of the Three Stooges!

Now, I am sure much is lost in the translation of Jim's belly-flop across the years as I tell it to you now, but, take it from me, it was about as hilarious as a four-year-old peashooter marksman could imagine. I whooped with joy, guffawed, and fell victim to my mother's stern warning, all at the same moment.

"'HAHAHAHA! . . . Gulp!" I swallowed a pea, right down the hatch, quicker than the time it takes to say it! And, in a moment of stunned realization, I remembered Mama's pronouncement of my doom:

"You're going to swallow a pea, and you'll DIE!"

Well, there it was. I was to die, rather instantly, I imagined—as quickly and surely as if I had been bitten by a black mamba. "You're going to swallow a pea, and you'll DIE!" she had said. She said it, I believed it, and that settled it. My Mama didn't lie. The hot flash of embarrassment turned to the cold truth in a blink of an eye.

My death watch started just that abruptly, and the injustice of a four-year-old life cut so short notwithstanding, I sat down on the edge of the old gray couch to face the Grim Reaper, (gasp!), alone!

Now, I had never died before, and never known anybody who had died, either. So, the whole prospect seemed pretty mysterious to me. I didn't seem to feel any different than just a few moments before, really. I wasn't choking, or in pain. All things considered, it wasn't so unpleasant. There were a few things I had heard about dying, however, and none of them good. For one thing, it wasn't supposed to be pleasant, and for another, I heard that people usually cried about it.

Oh, and another thing: I had heard somewhere that as you died, your whole life flashed in review before your eyes. But my life was only four years long, or short, as the case may be . . . so short I couldn't even conjure up a rerun! Failing the life-review thing, I guessed that what I needed to do was cry. Dying people cried, right? Everyone around them seemed to cry, anyway. And, maybe weeping a little would make me feel my way into this dying thing, for I still hadn't felt much different than before. Was this what it was like to die, I wondered? Huh, it was nothing like on TV!

I started to whimper, and then, warming to the whole mourning thing, I managed a little wail. Mama heard it, and came out of the kitchen, still swinging that damned spoon.

"What in the world is the matter with you?" she asked.

Stammering, I said, "I swallowed a . . . I swallowed a . . . I swallowed a . . . "

"YOU SWALLOWED A PEA!" Mama screamed, throwing the spoon down on the floor, and, driven by adrenaline, I suppose, grabbed me by the ankles with one hand, flipped me upside down, and started smacking me hard on the back with the other, trying to dislodge the pea! It was breathtaking, and scared the be-Jesus out of me! Now, this surely was more like what it meant for somebody to die!

Mama managed a few good whacks, and then had to sit down on the couch, heaving for breath. She acted like she was the one dying, and not me! What happened next surely came as the consequence of her considerable rationality: I didn't seem to be choking or turning blue in the face. No in extremis or death rattles. So, she quit, as abruptly as she had swung into action, retreated into the kitchen, and lit up a cigarette to calm her nerves. She must have concluded that the offending pea had gone down my esophagus, not my windpipe, and that I was not going to be any worse for the wear. But not a word to me, mind you! No Dr. Kildare or Dr. Marcus Welby or General Hospital words of reassurance, either. My God, the woman just abandoned me there, dying on the couch, ALONE! *Quelle horreur, mon petit chou!*

Oh, the inhumanity of it all! To be sentenced to death-by-dried-pea, thrashed upside down into a state of fright, and then abandoned like shipwrecked Robinson Crusoe to face my fate alone—now, that got me into a really good crying jag for a moment or two.

And then, it gradually came to me! Once I began to catch my breath back, I did a quick self-autopsy. Was I dead already? Nope. Sure didn't feel like it. Matter of fact, I didn't feel all that bad, really, and the rush had given me some energy to burn. I felt in my jeans pocket, and I still had some peas. The plastic peashooter was right there on the floor under the edge of the couch. Jim was romping outside like nothing special had happened, either. So, if this was what dying was like, it really wasn't half bad after all! And, if my moments were already numbered in some sort of perverse Calvinist scheme (the deep mysteries of which I would only plumb at a much later stage of consciousness), I decided that it was going to be better for me to keel over and croak outside having fun and playing my little ass off than for me to expire on the couch inside the house.

That's exactly what I did, Honey. I went outside, chasing Jim around the backyard, leaping and whooping like a goose on acid . . . and that's what I have been doing ever since—living rather happily on borrowed time!

"Hell Fire! My Meat's On Fire!"

Dad was a pipe smoker—all day, every day. He smoked a corn cob pipe with the same élan a concert musician plays his piccolo. Genuine Missouri Meershaums were his pipes of choice, crafted by hand in the same factory in Washington, Missouri since 1869. He bought them by the dozen, pulled out the filter in the stem of each pipe, and threw it away. He wanted the straight stuff when he smoked. Dad always said corn cob pipes burned cooler and sweeter than hardwood pipes. Dad's pipe tobacco of choice was Sir Walter Raleigh, in the orange and black tin can, as long as he could get it that way.

25

I used to play with his empties, flipping open the tin top to smell the sweet, aromatic reminder of the burley and bright leaf blend. Sir Walter's likeness graced every can, puffing a long stemmed pipe gracefully, with a faint Mona Lisa smile on his lips. I wondered how Sir Walter managed to smoke so much and not catch his impressive Elizabethan ruffed collar on fire. My father earned the nickname "Sir Walter" on the tobacco market and in the hardware store he managed, and endured all the standard jokes about his habit with good grace.

"Hey, Thed! (his given name was Thedford—but more about that, later). Have you got Sir Walter Raleigh in a can? (snicker, snicker, and a stifled snort). Well, you better let 'im out! It's dark in there!" (guffaw, guffaw).

My dad earned his nickname fair and square, smoking in every situation known to the pipe smoking world. Black and white snapshots of him smoking a pipe in uniform as an Army Air Corps Staff Sergeant during World War II were some of my childhood treasures. While he was stationed in Italy, I'm sure he and Mount Vesuvius enjoyed a good smoke together, the day he climbed up to the rim of the crater. Back home, he lit up before breakfast, and smoked his corn cob pipes throughout the day. Incredibly, he even smoked his pipe in the shower, lathering up with the soap first, his teeth clamped happily on the pipe stem, then holding the pipe away from his body as he shampooed his hair with the other hand, only to recommence smoking once his hair was clean. He was what tobacco men called a "dedicated smoker."

26

Dad smoked while he drove his car, too. His pride and joy was a powder blue '56 Buick Roadmaster Riviera four-door hardtop, the dashboard cluttered with smoked-out pipes and fresh ones waiting to be lit up. With the skill of a carnival juggler, he could knock the fire of a pipe out the little triangle window beside him, toss the empty on the dash, select a fresh pipe from his pocket, manipulate the Sir Walter tobacco into the bowl, strike a match from the matchbook he always carried, and puff it to life, all the while managing to drive like a bat out of hell on our narrow mountain roads with his little finger on the steering wheel.

Zipping up Turner Mountain one day, just Dad and I, he lost his pipe-lighting concentration telling me some tall tale from the tobacco market. Instead of tossing his finished pipe on the dashboard as usual, he absent-mindedly stuffed it into his sport coat pocket with about half a bowl of fire still in it. Chatting away, he had just put the match to his newly packed pipe, when his hands flew off the steering wheel, his foot sprang off the gas pedal, and he spit his pipe into the windshield, yelling like a banshee, "Hell fire! My meat's on fire! HELL FIRE! MY MEAT'S ON FIRE!!"

As small as I was, how I managed to wrestle a hurtling Buick Roadmaster to the side of that mountain road without plunging off a cliff, I will never know, while Dad thrashed and beat fire in his lap for all he was worth. The moment the car stopped, Dad threw the door open, vaulted himself out of the driver's seat, and did the damnedest chicken dance on the side of that mountain anyone has ever seen! "HELL FIRE, MY MEAT'S ON FIRE, MY MEAT'S ON F-I-I-I-RE! E-E-E-E-Y-O-O-OW!!"

By the time I got out of the car, he had shucked down his britches and torn off his smoking boxer shorts. Hell, his meat had been on fire! The embers from the half lit pipe had burned through the lining of his jacket pocket, through his britches pocket and lining, through the crotch of his boxers, and a red hot coal had dropped smack on the head of his John Thomas, raising a whale of a blister right on the "ped of his hecker"! Poor man!

To add insult to injury, Mama laughed at him about it. From time to time, I considered picking up the pipe smoking habit myself, but the memory of fried meat always kept me from it.

Raw Head and Bloody Bones

Grandma Dell, my maternal Great Grandmother, was a *raconteuse*. She was a self-taught mountain storyteller who had the gift to make anything she told entertaining. I never knew her. She was seven years old at the outbreak of the American Civil War (still known around home as "The Late Unpleasantness"), and enjoyed a good, long life, shuffling off this mortal coil in 1929 at the age of 76.

Elders around home tell me I am a lot like her. It must be the big mouth, I guess.

Mr. Sid Comer who used to be a county sheriff told me about how he loved to hear Grandma Dell tell stories. All the children, he said, huddled close around her as she spoke, so they wouldn't miss a word. My eldest aunt, Irene, told me

Grandma Dell taught herself to read, and that she read everything she could get her hands on—another trait we share. So, though she told familiar children's stories, her versions of them bore her own particular pronunciations of their names, unsullied by the conventional way of sounding them out. For example, Grandma Dell told about the boy from over yonder in Arabia who was walking along a beach, kicking up the sand. He stubbed his toe on a metal oil lamp, and he picked it up, then he rubbed it, and rubbed it, and rubbed it to clean it off, and . . . "UP POPPED THE GEN-EYE!" (the Genie from Aladdin and His Marvelous Lamp). Or there was this Little Swiss Girl who lived up the side of the mountain with her Granddaddy, (you know the story, don't ye?), how the little girl played and played with that Little Boy Peter who herded goats, and finally taught that Puny Girl how to walk again: "HEE-dee-eye!" (Heidi, of course). And, then, her favorite was the Eye-talian tale about the lonely old man who carved a Wooden Puppet Boy out of a tree limb so well that the Puppet came to life, and became the old man's son: "Pin-NOCK-ee-o" (Pinnochio). Nothing ignorant about Grandma Dell—she just pronounced things the way they looked to her. The children for whom she spun her tales were spellbound, begging for more.

She loved names. Her own name was Aradella Hamlin Martin. She named her three sons, my Grandfather and his two brothers, Thomas Hamlin Martin, Newton Jasper Martin, and, the youngest, Richard Vestal Martin: "Tom," "Newt," and (Wait for it!) . . . "Coot," of all things! How you get from a perfectly dignified name like Richard Vestal to "Coot Martin" is beyond me. Maybe it was my Great Uncle Coot's peculiarity that marked him with a nickname hard to shake.

Aunt Irene said the mean Stanley boys made fun of the Martin men by chanting an ugly little rhyme as she and they traveled on the bus to school. The Stanleys would mock Irene, saying loud enough for everybody to hear over the roar of the old bus engine:

"Newt Martin went a-fartin' to get a bail of hay;

"Coot Martin came a-fartin', and BLEW IT ALL AWAY!" (Cue the gales of laughter).

Irene said it made her mad enough to spit that she couldn't ever make up a rhyme with "Stanley" in it!

Grandma Dell loved her youngest son, but couldn't understand why he refused to come to church meeting once he became an adult—nearly ever, except for a funeral. He knew his Bible lid-to-lid. He just had no use for the congregation. It must have been the way she humiliated him in church as a teenager, when he had to go with his Mam and his Pap. Grandma Dell, like all the Martins, attended the Campbellite Church at Salem Fork. But in her heart, she was a "shouting Methodist" until the day she died. At the end of the service, when repentant sinners came down the aisle of the church to join, Irene said Grandma Dell would rise up in her pew, slap and pop her hands together, and cry out,

"Coot! Oh, Lordy, Coot! Hey, Lordy, Coot! When're ye gonna come over? Oh, Lordy, Coot!"

I suspect that was enough to give Uncle Coot a bellyful of religion for a lifetime.

She was ahead of her time in one respect, at least. Mr. Sid and Aunt Irene agreed that she was the most humane story-teller they ever knew. Mountain yarn spinners had a set of stock characters that showed up in nearly every repertoire. They were largely drawn from the "Jack Tales," an Appalachian folklore tradition that hearkens back to the thirteenth century in the Old Country. One set of such stories in the Southern U.S. that probably came over with Sir Walter Raleigh and other English explorers was "Raw Head and Bloody Bones," cautionary tales about two hobgoblins, told by adults to scare the hell out of children and make them mind.

Most storytellers would say that Raw Head and Bloody Bones lived under the stairs, or in a cupboard in the shadows. Raw Head was the mean one. Bad children who disobeyed their parents or used bad words would get a nighttime visit from him, a boogerman with blood running down his face, who lived on a pile of the bones of girls and boys who wouldn't mind. Bloody Bones was Raw Head's sidekick, who snatched up kids and stuffed them in a burlap sack, to carry them back to their lair under the stairs. Particularly sadistic tale tellers brought the evil pair smack into the children's bedrooms, saying that they lived right under their beds, ready to grab a child by the ankle if he tried to get up in the night, or allowed so much as a hand to droop over the bedside! Those stories traumatized many a kid in those days, and "young uns" would often rather wet the bed at night than risk a run to the Johnny house outdoors.

Grandma Dell would have none of that meanness. She loved children, and though she told some of the same stories about Raw Head and Bloody Bones, on her own authority, she assured the girls and boys that neither of these "boogers" lived in the house. "Naw, Honey," she'd say. They lived 'way down at the edge of the woods, below the pasture, so that children wouldn't risk running away from home, or going into the forest after nightfall. All the children she knew, Grandma Dell said to her young audiences, were good anyway, and, Lordy, nobody had any reason to fear Rawhead and Bloody Bones as long as they minded their parents and said their prayers before going to bed. Instead of leaving them with nightmares, she populated their dreams with the boy with the magic lamp, and the little Swiss girl who lived with her Granddaddy, and visions of "Eye-talian" Geppetto hugging his little wooden boy.

I wish I were half the storyteller she was.

Sweet dreams.

Buried Alive

I can't remember a time I didn't call my grandmother "Bessie." Other grandkids called their mother's mother "Grandma," or "Grandmama," or "Meemaw." Not any of Bessie Venable Martin's grandchildren. All four of us called her, "Bessie." Just like all of us called her husband, our mother's father, "Tom," instead of the generic "Grandpa." No disrespect intended, and none taken! My cousins and I loved and respected her for her wise love and generous acceptance of us, just as we were.

Bessie lived in the big house up beyond the cow pasture next door to my home. When my Dad married my Mama, Bessie and Tom gave them an acre of land beside their property where we came to live. I thought "Bessie's House" was the greatest place on earth—and why wouldn't I? She doted on me, and let me get away with murder—kid-style, of course (or so I thought).

Bessie had chickens: Rhode Island Reds. She had three little chicken houses, complete with nesting boxes, though the hens laid eggs most anywhere they liked—up in the hayloft of the barn, or on the back porch of the house. She kept 150 hens and a single rooster. That was a heavenly arrangement for a small boy with a good dirt-clod throwing arm.

Did you know that a clod of dry, red clay will explode like a hand grenade when it hits the ground in the midst of a flock of pullets? And, that to a rascally little boy's ears, the sound of a dozen chickens in full panic from dirt clods is better than music, and the sight of red hens running helter-skelter is better than Saturday morning cartoons on TV? Well, that is the dad-gummed truth!

After the spring plowing to plant tobacco, strawberries, and the vegetable garden, a veritable arsenal of missiles simply rolled up out of the ground, just begging to be thrown at those gullible chickens. And the chickens seemed to collude with me in the whole game, since after a lapse of just a few minutes, all the poultry that had flogged each other and raised a clucking racket as clods exploded in their midst, ambled back into range again.

Uncle Ray, Bessie's youngest and my childhood nemesis, had no patience with my shenanigans. He demanded justice from his mother every time he caught me clodding the chickens in the yard, saying, "Whip him, Mama! Whip him right now! He's been clodding the chickens all afternoon, and he's gonna get 'em so they won't lay or even roost! Whip him right now!"

My grandmother Bessie would say, "I don't reckon I will. He's a right cute kid." That sent Ray into a snit, stomping off out of sight for a while. Whereupon I immediately recommenced my bombardment of the pullets.

That very scenario had just played itself out on a Spring afternoon, chapter and verse. I had indeed clodded the chickens beside the house, under the tall pear tree. Ray had caught me, and called Bessie out of her kitchen where she was cooking supper. "Whip him, Mama!" he pleaded, "Whip him right now! He's gonna kill those chickens!" To which she replied, as she always did with a wry little grin on her face, "No, I don't reckon I will. He's a right cute kid." She turned around and went back into the kitchen to finish the cornbread. Disgusted, Ray swung up into the seat of his old, red Allis Chalmers tractor, and chugged off to cool his temper.

And I? Well, you know what I did! In a moment of triumph over Uncle Ray, I picked up another dirt clod, cocked back my arm, and let fly! But just as soon as that clod left the palm of my hand, I knew something was seriously wrong with it! By touch, having launched untold dozens of missiles at the chickens in fun and play, I knew this one didn't feel right—Oh My God, it wasn't a dirt clod at all! It was a quartz rock, cloaked in dry red clay, and as the rock arced along its deadly path, I watched in horror, unable to bring it back!

If I had truly aimed it, rather than just pitching it towards a knot of hens, I could not have been more certain of the result. That rock, flying through the air like it was in slow motion, struck the side of a pullet's head with a sickening "pop." She rolled over and over, landing on her back, kicked twice in the air, and then . . . nothing! I had hit and killed one of Bessie's chickens! My face burnt red with shame and fear, as I rushed up and tugged on the scaly yellow feet of a motionless victim of my folly! I felt sick!

Now, the very first thing I did was to whirl around and look for Ray, to see if he had witnessed my crime. But he was no-where in sight. Matter of fact, no one was around at all. So, being the good Christian kid I was, I decided to drag off the evidence and hide the body. Oh, how awful those minutes were! The pullet was heavy, dead weight, so to speak. I pulled her corpse along to the edge of the woods where the soil was loamy and loose, loose enough that I could scoop out a make-shift grave with my bare hands. As I buried the evidence of my poultry-cide, I prayed every prayer I knew from Sunday School, and recited all the Bible verses we had to memorize— John 3:16, Psalm 23, and the Ten Commandments! Oh, how I prayed and pleaded with God to bring that chicken back to life! I even recited all 27 books of the New Testament, which we had to learn by heart, too, but to no avail. I arranged moss over the grave, tried to dry my tears, and turned to trudge away, sorrowing, from the grave, guilty sinner that I was . . . .

And then, I heard it! "Rustle, rustle . . . rustle, rustle, rustle!" Turning back, I saw the loose moss and dirt atop the grave moving! Oh, Jesus! I had buried that poor chicken ALIVE! But God had answered my prayers, and had resurrected that pullet from the dead—and my hopes of getting away with the crime along with it!

Thanking God and Jesus, I dug up that little hen like a madman, praising heaven, and promising to go for six weeks (well, maybe four) of Sunday School without complaint, since I had such absolute proof of God's grace. I brushed off her rust red feathers, and then witnessed the awful truth of what I had done. Yes, I had only knocked the pullet unconscious with the quartz rock, and she had come to, to live again. But, as the old folks used to say, she wasn't quite right in the head.

I had hit the pullet so hard that it must have spun her birdbrain around. She couldn't walk forward or backward any more. All she could do was go side-to-side, like a crab. And, as I began to nurse her, and tried to feed and water her, I saw that she had no spatial comprehension any more, either. She couldn't hit what she aimed at, or dip her beak into water without a struggle. So, there it was. God had given me a second chance, and made me as responsible for that chicken as if it were my own special needs child.

Oh, how I dedicated myself to her upkeep! I came up through the pasture two times a day, morning and evening, to hand feed and water my chicken. She was the cleanest hen you ever saw, 'cause I brushed and arranged her feathers every night as I put her up on her roost. I even named her after my Aunt Joyce (which Joyce didn't seem to appreciate very much. Having a chicken named for you is not the greatest "get" in the world, you know). If a boy could ever to be said to love a chicken, I guess I loved Joyce the Hen. She would follow me sideways through the barnyard, like a puppy.

Six months into my labors on Joyce the Hen's behalf, something went wrong, and she really did die, this time. I cried. I went to Bessie and asked her for a shovel. She went with me down to the edge of the woods, where the soil is loose, and I dug Joyce a little grave. After burying her, and planting a nice field stone at the head of her grave, Bessie asked if I wanted to say a few words over my hen. Yes, I said, I did. It was all very proper and in good order, she thought.

As we walked back to her house, Bessie said, sort of absently to no one in particular (but to me, of course), "Well, I'm sort of glad it all ended this way. After you hit that pullet in the head with a rock, and then brought her back with you alive from where you buried her the first time, I thought you were going to near about work yourself to death taking care of her."

"......(!)......"

"You saw what I did?" I said, with a catch in my throat.

"Sure did. I saw it all out of the kitchen window."

Bessie let the silence do the talking as we walked back to her house from the edge of the woods. Silence often gets the job done a lot better than chin music. Then, all full of grace, she turned towards me and opened her arms.

"Never mind, Honey," she said. "You're still a right cute kid."

Pig Milk

Watch what you tell a child. No telling what that child will make of what you say! Everybody's grandmother hung the moon, I guess, or at least that's what we all think. In the case of my grandmother, Bessie Venable Martin, I have no doubt she did, really and truly. Oh, yes, she spoiled me more than she should. I can still hear her say, "Honey, I think you're a right cute kid!" But there was a lot more to her than that.

Mama had a "nervous condition," or at least that's what they called it. She would lie down on the couch in the living room, and tell me to go on to Bessie's House so she could get some rest. That was fine with me! My favorite place was right beside Bessie, whatever she was doing. As many times as I surely got in her way and doubled her work, it never seemed to bother her. And she taught me so many things! Like how to get up the eggs her Rhode Island Red hens laid. Bessie showed me where to find the nests in the bed of the old wagon, in the briar bushes safe from the foxes, and then 'way up in the hayloft of the barn! Now, you never take away all the eggs. You have to leave at least one egg in each nest, so the hen will go back tomorrow and lay some more.

I got a brand new pair of Oshkosh B'Gosh red corduroy bibbed overalls when I was barely six, and I had to show them to Bessie! Something that pretty just had to be shared with the best person in my life! So I ran up through the cow pasture with the zip-zip-swishing sound of scraping corduroy at every stride, raced past gentle, doe-eyed old Bossy, the brown Jersey cow with one horn, and into the yard of Bessie's House.

"Bessie! Bessie!" I hollered. No reply.

Since she wasn't right at hand, and it was between 5 p.m. and supper—prime egg-collecting time—I thought, "Won't Bessie be happy if I go ahead and get up the eggs for her! I can show her my pretty red overalls at the same time I present her with all the eggs!" What a plan!

So, I sought out all the nests I knew, with Mutt the Collie dog attending my every step, collecting all but the last egg from each nest, just like Bessie had taught me. In all, I got up five fresh brown eggs without dirtying up my new britches! I knew I couldn't manage to carry all five eggs in my six-year-old hands without dropping some of them, so I put two eggs in each of my brand new red overall pockets, and carried one in my left hand. I had to walk carefully, because my pockets were slam-jammed full of eggs. As I got up to the house, I saw Bessie working in her kitchen. Wasn't she going to be surprised! I waddled up to the three big steps leading to the kitchen door, and swung my foot up.

"Ker-r-r-a-a-a-ck!" went the first egg—then "ker-r-r-ack!" again! Both eggs in my right pocket broke! In desperation and panic, I stepped up with my other foot. Then, loud as the discharge of a cap pistol, "Ker-r-r-a-a-a-ck! Ker-r-r-a-a-a-ck!" two more times! Noooo! I had busted four eggs in the pockets of my new Oshkosh B'Gosh red corduroy overalls, and liquid chicken was running down the inside of my britches legs! I wailed like a motherless child!

Bessie heard me and rushed to the door. She swung open the screen. "Honey, what in the world!" she said.

"Oh, Bessie, noooo!" I continued to wail. "I wanted to show you my new red overalls (sniff!), and when I didn't see you I got up the eggs for you and put two in each pocket (sniff!)—but I BUSTED 'EM ALL climbing the steps, and now I have RUINED my new britches, and Mama is gonna whip me for sure!" Then, with a little spasm I couldn't control, I lost my grip on the last egg, the one in my hand, and it fell like Humpty Dumpty right onto the kitchen step, and broke all over the place. I let out another self-pitying wail!

"Now, never you mind about the eggs, Honey. You just come into Bessie's kitchen, and I'll take your new britches and wash 'em out, so your Mama will never need to know a thing about it, y'hear?" Then, she spoke the most magical words of my childhood: "You know," she said, "I think you're a right cute kid!"

So, Bessie wiped down my legs with a dish rag, got me a pair of my Grandpa Tom's 'way too big boxer shorts to wear, put me up on top of her wooden meal chest with a fine mellow pear to eat, and cranked up the washing machine with the wringer on top that sat on her back porch. Oh, we talked about everything—chickens, and her flogging rooster, and how funny Mutt the dog was, and had I heard the woodpeckers knocking and knocking up in the trees? Bessie washed the beautiful red overalls, and put them through the wringer of the washing machine twice to get them as dry as she could before she hung them out on the clothesline to finish drying. I sat there in my granddad's too big boxer shorts, content to munch on my pear, while Bessie got supper ready for Tom, Uncle Ray, and me. As she cooked on her wood stove, she hummed and sang her favorite church hymn, "I Will Arise and Go To Jesus." Bessie had a way of making things go right, even when they had gone horribly wrong.

Her kitchen was permeated by decades of good Southern cooking. The meal chest was right beside her wood stove under the kitchen window. A mere yard and a half separated the cooking area from the dining room table, surrounded by six chairs. The whole place smelled of bacon drippings, boiled turnips, the unmistakable aroma of her stove top corn pone, fried up in a black iron skillet, and, of course, the tang of homemade buttermilk. Bessie liked to cook with buttermilk a lot.

Like most women of her time, Bessie churned her own butter from milk dispensed by Ol' Bossy the cow. Mutt and I would follow her down to the stable to milk, going down below the hog pen where the pigs Henry and Henrietta lived and ate slop. I was fastidious for a little boy, and didn't care much for the way those pigs rolled their bellies in the mud, but Bessie said it felt good and cool to them, so, okay. Ol' Bossey provided about a bucket and a half of rich milk a day. On churning day, Bessie brought out the large stoneware churn, poured the milk she had saved up in the spring house to keep it fresh, ran the wooden dasher through the hole in the churn's wooden lid, and started pounding away. I knew I didn't have the patience for churning. It took 'way too long for a little boy. But Bessie had patience by the bushel. She sat there hour on hour, churning and humming "I will arise and go to Jesus/He will embrace me in his arms/In the arms of my Dear Savior/Oh! There are ten thousand charms!"

At some point, like sorcery, butter would form in the churn. Bessie would scoop out the wonderful, pastel yellow butter, wrap it in cheesecloth, and stick it in the icebox before pressing it into a butter mold. Flakes of butter swirled around in the richest of the leftover milk that she poured out into a big glass screw top container. That was the buttermilk she and my Dad loved to drink right out of the icebox. The rest of the leftover milk, watery with a blue tint to it, wasn't fit to keep. She called it "pig milk," and she poured it straight from the churn into the slop bucket situated behind the wood stove, full of all sorts of leavings for the pigs.

Now, somewhere between the prized buttermilk and the throwaway blue milk, I got deeply confused. What she meant was that the slop bucket milk wasn't fit for anything else but feeding Henry and Henrietta, the big black hogs. She called it "pig milk," though, and in my child mind, I confused buttermilk that came from the cow, with sow's milk that came from a pig. I had never seen anybody actually milk a pig, but a sow had teats. I had seen 'em, row on row, dragging in the mud, leaking milk when the sow had little piglets! Perhaps there was some nefarious nighttime ritual when folks went down to the hog pen with a stool, and milked their sows under cover of darkness so decent people wouldn't have to watch the atrocity. I didn't know. All I could think of when Bessie and my Dad turned up a cold glass of buttermilk at the supper table was the sight of that big black sow's teats marinating in the mud and poop—and, oh, the smell! That must be the "pig milk" Bessie talked about (ugh!)! How could human beings bear to drink such stuff as "pig milk"? What Bessie meant to say and what she actually said got crossed up in my delicate sensibilities.

A word to the wise: a child is a fundamentalist before metamorphosis. Children are helplessly literal. Hadn't Bessie said "pig milk" wasn't fit for anything but slopping the hogs? And now she and Dad were swigging down the sour tasting stuff, and even offering me a swallow of it?

Oh, no! Oh, hell no! No "pig milk" for this child o' God!

Aunt Kizzie's Arithmetic

In the latter years of her long, long life, Aunt Kizzie got a restricted driver's license. Aunt Kizzie was the widow of my Great Uncle Newt. She and my Grandma Bessie, her sister-in-law, had lived cheek-by-jowl for years in the rambling, Victorian-style house Uncle Newt and my Grandpa Tom had built together while they ran Martin's Store at the Rusk Crossroads. Cohabitation lasted until Grandpa finally built his family a home of their own across the road. Since Uncle Newt preceded her in death by many years, and since they were childless, Aunt Kizzie lived alone.

But back in the day, the old house buzzed with activity. Mama, her sisters, and her little brother were all born in that house. The quiet decorum Aunt Kizzie (short for "Kizziah") loved was routinely shattered by the squeals, fusses, and mini-dramas every growing family with small children knows about all too well. Like the time Mama and her elder sister Irene were watching their baby brother Ray in the upstairs room over the back porch. It was summer, and the window was open to admit a breeze. While they weren't looking, Baby Ray climbed up on the window sill in a flash, letting out a little boy chuckle as he began to tumble head-first to his certain death on the hard ground so far below—but Irene lunged and grabbed him by the diaper in a heroic snatch-and-grab that surely saved Ray's life. Aunt Kizzie and Bessie hustled the nursery down to the ground floor after that little debacle!

Then, there was Great Grand Uncle Bill—William R. Martin. Uncle Bill, a veteran of the War Between the States, lived in a room in that house, too, and contributed his soldier's pension to the household kitty. Uncle Bill was a legend of sorts. He had enlisted in the North Carolina militia at the outbreak of the war in 1861 by lying about his age. He claimed he was 18, but he was younger. When North Carolina state troops became nationalized by the Confederacy, his unit, originally the 11th Volunteers, became the 21st North Carolina Infantry Regiment—a unit in General Thomas J. "Stonewall" Jackson's Foot Cavalry that terrorized Yankee troops throughout the conflict. The Surry County boys formed Company H, "The Mountain Tigers." Uncle Bill served in every major campaign in the Eastern Theater of the war: among them, First and Second Bull Run (or "First and Second Manassas" as Confederates called 'em), Cross Keys, Front Royal, and First Winchester in the Shenandoah Valley, the Seven Days Battles outside

Richmond, Fredericksburg, Chancellorsville, and Gettysburg, where 28 percent of their 436 troops were listed as casualties. General Robert E. Lee, supreme commander of the Army of Northern Virginia, affectionately called the 21st North Carolina and its twin unit, the 21st Georgia, his "two twenty-ones." As other officers died in combat or from disease, Uncle Bill rose in rank, first as a second lieutenant, then first lieutenant, and finally as captain. He was wounded in the hand at Second Fredericksburg, and survived treatment in the sprawling, septic environs of Richmond's Chimborazo Hospital, after which he returned to serve with the 21st North Carolina until its surrender at Appomattox Courthouse in April 1865. Uncle Bill was one of 6 surviving officers who led 117 men during the surrender, only 40 of whom were still armed.

Family legend said that Uncle Bill's hair turned white due to the horrors of the war. Perhaps it did, but if so, he was a white-haired young adult at the end of hostilities. People used to call him "Colonel" as a way of honoring his service.

Because of Uncle Bill's notoriety, men visited him often in the big house. It was common knowledge that he loved the flavor of baked opossum, and when one was trapped in the neighborhood, it was brought to Uncle Bill alive as a gift. Since Aunt Kizzie didn't like to cook, the chore fell to my Grandma Bessie, who detested the whole exercise. For one thing, the 'possum had to be kept for a week in a barrel out behind the house and fed cornmeal to leach out the gamey taste. Then Bessie had to kill the varmint, singe the hair off of it, skin it, and bake it in a pan with sweet 'taters. She told me it was a greasy mess, and because Uncle Bill liked it so much, he always ate like a hog, got sick with a belly ache, and then she had to tend him while he recovered. As often as she could, Bessie would take the 'possums the men gave Uncle Bill, and set them loose behind his back rather than suffer through the whole ordeal.

Uncle Bill doted on my Mama, Hazel. Matter of fact, Irene told me she had her feelings hurt a little bit over it, since Uncle Bill was always going on about how pretty Mama was. Every time he saw Mama, Uncle Bill had a gift for her: a shiny, silver dime! And every time, Mama had a little kiss on the cheek for Uncle Bill.

Aunt Kizzie was a pack rat. She never threw anything away, it seemed. Thanks to her, my cousins and I found letters and magazines, old ads from Martin's Store, and handwritten love notes shared between Aunt Bet and her suitors (one particularly juicy one was from a man named Brinkley: "Up the Willow and Down the Pine/Wish to the Lord that You was Mine!"). I suppose she couldn't let go of the memories of her beloved Newt and the sounds of laughter in the old house, long after it was all gone.

But, back to the restricted driver's license. That happened, according to my Aunt Irene, when Aunt Kizzie nearly ran a state trooper into the side ditch because she had trouble seeing—"presbyopia," or "old person's eyes," they called it. After that little escapade, Aunt Kizzie was limited to a five mile radius. That was enough to permit her to drive to Dobson for groceries, go to the drug store, and see her doctor at the clinic. It also allowed her to make it back and forth to church on Sunday.

But one fine Spring day, a Mount Airy Police Officer saw Aunt Kizzie's Bellaire Chevrolet weaving back and forth on Main Street near Harrison's Dress Shop. He pulled her over, asking for her license, please ma'am. When he saw the five mile radius restriction on her license, the officer said, a little cattily, "How's your arithmetic, Ma'am? You can count, can't you?"

A Little Aside on Hillbilly Mathematics

Now, Gentle Reader, I was often taken aback by the wiles of hillbilly math. For example, when my Grandpa Sprinkle heard that I was going away to college, he pulled me aside and asked, "Steve, now yer goin' to take arithmetic in that college, aren't ye?"

"Sure will, Grandpa. Why?"

"Well, boy, yer gonna take classes from smart people, Perfessers, ain't ye?"

"That's right, Grandpa."

"Well then, ask them smart Perfessers of yours if they know how to square a circle. You know how to square a circle, don't ye?"

"I don't know as I do, Grandpa. I never learned the formula for squaring a circle in geometry."

His eyes glittered as he revealed the hidden truth that even college professors of mathematics don't know. "It's easy to square a circle, boy! You just take a 4X4, and cram it up a bull's ass!" (Grandpa rolls off his chair laughing at me).

Now, back to Aunt Kizzie and the Mount Airy Policeman

"Why, yes, of course, Officer," Aunt Kizzie said. "I believe my arithmetic is pretty good."

"Now, Ma'am, you do know that you have a five mile restriction on this license, and that Mount Airy is 12 miles from where you live, don't you?"

"Oh, why, yes," she said, as pleasantly as she could.

"Now, Mrs. Martin, if you can count, you know that you are seven miles beyond your restriction. How do you explain that?"

"Well, Officer, I can explain it well enough. I know I have a five mile restriction, so I simply didn't drive for a whole week, and saved up 35 miles!"

The policeman stifled his guffaw, and she got off with a warning.

Scrooge and Scrooge Jr.

My Uncle Ray was a piece of work. His canned response to Christmas was enough to make Bob Cratchit cringe: "Bah! Humbug!" Easter, Halloween, all the other gift-giving holidays: "Bah! Humbug!"

"Scrooge" was a verb to Uncle Ray: "to Scrooge," meant "by all means necessary, squeeze the nickel until the buffalo farts." One Halloween, I knocked on his door for Trick-or-Treat. The porch light snapped on, Ray opened the porch door, took one look at me, and retreated into the house. I heard his big brogans clumping up the hall toward the door. I opened my sack, expectantly.

"Bah! Humbug!" he grumbled. "Trick or Treat your own self!" Ray dropped a whole stick of firewood into my goodie sack, busting up all my cookies and candy. "Wham!" The door shut hard. End of transaction.

Christmas was Uncle Ray's *pièce de résistance.* His dark humor abounded when the multicolored lights began to wink on and off on holiday trees and rooflines. When he gave me a present for Christmas, I knew he always had an ulterior motive. As a tiny kid, I got so excited because Ray had wrapped up a present all for me! I tore open the shiny paper and found . . . (to my bewilderment) a Do-It-Yourself Radio Kit from Western Electric: scores of bits, pieces and wires, and a big clear plastic dial I had not the first idea of what to do with. I was into just about anything else other than technical things, and Ray knew it. I wasn't nearly butch enough for electronics. So, when I reacted as he predicted, and just let the Radio Kit lie there in its box a couple of days, he took it home for himself—as he had intended all along. "Bah! Humbug!"

My Boston Terrier, Jim, gave Uncle Ray an idea. He never liked my dog, and Jim returned the compliment. Ray learned that the Dobson Insurance Company was offering a new product: Dog Bite Insurance. He bought a policy, and trooped down the road through the cow pasture to our house to collect. We heard terrible snarls coming out of our garage, so I rushed out to see what the hell was going on. Ray had backed Jim dog into a corner, and was experimentally poking his finger in a wee bit shy of Jim's under bite, sort of like a bear testing the resolve of bees in a hive, just to see if he could get nipped a tiny bit to justify his new policy. Jim curled up his lips and made a horrible racket, but never bit him—not even close, much to Ray's chagrin. "Bah!" Ray said. "Foiled again!"

Uncle Ray had a sort of "W.C. Fields" opinion of kids. "Ah, yes, my little wooden head," Fields would grump, "I love the patter of little feet around the house. There's nothing like having a midget for a butler." That was Ray. But over time, I learned he was a paper tiger. He just had an oddball way of expressing that he liked you.

I broke through by picking up his trademark, smart alecky remark, and tossing it right back at him. We volleyed "Bah! Humbug!" back and forth like tennis champions on the court at Wimbledon. Ray's façade cracked and he grinned. He couldn't help himself. "Me Scrooge," he said, pointing to himself. Then, pointing back at me, "You Scrooge Jr." I guess he had seen too many Tarzan movies.

The Freedom Sunshine Company

Growing older improved both my Uncle Ray and me. Often when people mature, they can appreciate things in others they didn't see or understand in them before. That was certainly the case with my estimation of Uncle Ray. Isn't that odd? As we grow up, the people around us seem to get better.

Ray always seemed to like most animals a good deal more than he liked people. He had a way with four-footed souls that was evident to anybody. His dogs seemed to know him personally, and he them. Ray always said that the quality he appreciated in dogs was that, unlike human beings, they never barked unless they had something to say.

Ray's dog Croppy was legendary in the family. Croppy was a black and white mixed breed that he reared from a pup. It was almost as if those two could read each other's minds. Croppy instinctively knew what Ray wanted him to do, as if the communication between them was telepathic. Spooky! When Croppy died of old age, Ray was practically inconsolable. The family wondered whether he would ever have another dog, because the pain of losing Croppy had been so great.

Then, Mutt came along, and it was love at first bark. Mutt was a beautiful purebred Collie, with long, golden and white fur that shimmered in the sun while he trotted along behind Ray, and a distinctive Collie face full of character, like Lassie on the television series. His resemblance with the celebrity Collie was uncanny, actually. Now, we know that the supposedly female Lassie was actually a set of successive males—just like Mutt.

Mutt learned the farm routine from Ray quickly, and as he grew into full doghood, he always seemed to appear in the right place at the right time: beside Ray in the morning as he checked the barn and readied the tractor for the day; accompanying my Grandmother Bessie as she first went to the stables to milk the cow, and then along with her to get up the eggs the chickens had laid the night before; and finally stationing himself at the head of the path that led to my house to meet me after school. Ray was generous with Mutt. He was never jealous when his dog liked somebody else.

Mutt went down in the annals of my maternal grandparents' family as the best dog they had ever known. He earned this regard the day he stopped Bessie from walking down the path to slop the hogs, and physically pushed her to the side as he got between her and a coiled copperhead, ready to strike when she passed by. Mutt killed the snake, and became a fable of canine quality.

It was so hard to lose Mutt! That's one thing life on a farm teaches: all life is fleeting, and whatever immortality we do have comes from the memories we treasure of those we have loved. None was more beloved on the farm than Mutt. As careful as he always was crossing the road in front of the house, someone must have aimed to hit him. We heard the shriek, and the fast getaway of the vehicle, headed hell bent for leather up the mountain. Ray got to his dog first. He picked up Mutt's broken body, and carried him under the shade of the trees. Nothing could be done to save him. We all knew it. Ray wouldn't leave him, cradling and stroking his magnificent head in his lap until the vet came, and then right until the end. We knew to let Ray alone with his grief. Somewhere on the back part of the land, away from prying eyes, Ray laid Mutt to rest in the red velvet earth. He never owned another dog.

But a horse was another story. Maud was a massive, rusty-red mare, with a white blaze down her great fore-head, a blonde mane, and hooves as large as dinner plates. No tell-ing how many hundred pounds she weighed—maybe half a ton. Maud was bred to plow, a skill most needed on small farms in the foothill country.

Looking back on Ray's relationship with that colossal mare, I suppose Mutt's soul transmigrated into her. Ray would get her out of the stable, and she would follow him down to the fields as if she were a dog.

"Hey, Hoss!" Ray would say. "Hey, Hoss!" And Maud would whinny in reply, toss her head, and rumble her satisfaction down deep in her chest. Season in and season out, Ray and Maud plowed the places the old Allis Chalmers tractor couldn't reach. She and he hauled logs, pulled the hay rake over the cut hay in the late summer, and pulled tons of harvested corn and towers of hay bales stacked by Ray and my Granddad Tom in the stout wooden wagon kept under the barn shed. "Hey, Hoss! Hey, Hoss! Gee! (right turn), Haw! (left turn)," and "Come about!" Alexander the Great never loved Bucephalus more than Ray loved Maud.

Ray grew quieter as the years passed. His love of animals intensified. He never married. Yet, his willing spirit and mechanical skill at repairing lawnmowers and hot water heaters kept the widow women of Salem Fork trimming their yards and washing the dishes for decades—all at no charge, so far as I ever heard. Vern and Nolie and Versie and Reba all called him "blessed."

Don't mistake Ray for a hermit or a misanthrope, however. He had an offbeat, even radical side not very many people were allowed to see. That is why the hippies at the Freedom Sunshine Company came to like him so much. They and he had a great deal in common, as it turned out.

The Freedom Sunshine Company was a commune of free thinkers who had "gone back to the land to set their souls free" in the sixties. They bought a large tract of land up the mountain in a secluded valley, and their property could only be accessed on foot, by horse, or by motorcycle. They were the real deal: men in tie-dyes with long hair and beards, braless women, and lots of kids. There must have been 30 folks or more living in the commune at its height. In their effort to get back to the land, they chose to live a primitive, self-sustaining life far away from the rat race of "success" and "materialism." Their contact with the outer world was limited to trips into town for necessities, or to sell their produce. As I heard it, they owned only a single radio. Monks in the Middle Ages had nothing on them!

Ray met some of the men the day they stopped by the farm and asked if they could buy the horse drawn, rusty hay rake sitting in the field by the roadside.

"No," Ray told them, "it's not for sale. But I will give it to you for nothing."

Within a day or two, a couple of their leaders came by again to ask if Ray would do them the honor of coming to Freedom Sunshine for dinner. Ray accepted, and became one of the very few locals the hippies gave full access anytime he wanted to visit. It helped that Ray had a wealth of farming and technical knowledge to share with his new friends, typical of the generosity that was the best side of my Uncle's character. There is no telling if the commune would have folded without Ray. Maybe so, maybe not. All I know is that he really enjoyed going up to see them, to learn and to share what he knew that might be of use to them—about seeds and transplanting, soils and fertilizer, fruit trees and grapevines, bees, engine repair, livestock and poultry, and the wonderful ways of draft horses.

I like to think that Uncle Ray was the Salem Fork community's Squanto to their Massachusetts Bay Colony. There was considerable synergy between them.

You might say he was our Original Hippy, dressed out in dungarees, lace-up brogans, and topped off with a red Allis

Chalmers ball cap. What he did counted more than anything he had to say. It was his authentic presence that mattered, at the Freedom Sunshine Company, and wherever else he went. After all, like his beloved dogs, Ray never barked unless he had something to say.

Hillbilly Grotesquerie

Grotesquerie, n.: *The quality of being grotesque, or ogre-ish; a monstrosity, or something bizarre enough to be on display, as in a "sideshow grotesquerie" you might pay a quarter or two to see at a carnival.*

When the Fair came to Mount Airy in the Fall, I was first in line to be admitted. I came to stare at all the people! Situated at the foot of the Blue Ridge Mountains, Mount Airy was a magnet for people from the foothills and the high mountains at Fair Time. The Surry County Agricultural Fair had everything—livestock (Pigs! I loved the pigs! Especially the piglet races . . . You know, Hamlet vs. Pork Chop vs. Tammy Swinette!); 4-H exhibits (I was a dedicated 4-H'er); the Midway, with its games of chance and skill nobody ever won, and the rides, the rides, the glorious rides; a confiscated liquor still, on display by the Revenuers to discourage manufacture and sale of non-tax paid white lightning (the only effect of which I ever saw was to give young men big ideas for how to make some quick cash); food booths with all manner of things frying and sizzling, salty and sour and sweet (Elephant Ears, turkey drumsticks, funnel cakes, and fried pickles); and, of course, the carnival sideshows!

The sideshows got everybody's last quarter. There was Pin Head, The World's Tiniest Horse, The World's Most Gi-normous Crocodile from the River Nile, Fatima, the Snake-woman, The Ubiquitous Sword-swallower, The Bearded Lady, and The Amazing Blockhead who could drive nails up his nose into his cranium with a hammer ("Go ahead and touch the hammer, Boy, and tell 'em that it's real!")!

I can still hear the Barker's chant in my little boy imagination:

"Hurry! Hurry! Hurry! Right this way, Ladies and Gentle-men!—(Move along, Sonny, ya' bother me!)—Right this way! Only one thin quarter, two bits of a dollar will admit you to see The Amazing Fatima, the Snake-Woman! She wriggles, she twists, she crawls on her belly like a Rep-tile! Hurry! Hurry! Hurry!"

And as you hesitated one last time, the Barker would purr, "Don't worry about your friends, . . . they're already in-side!"

There were the ever-popular Hootchie-Coochie Shows, too, just off the Midway, down the back alley. Men with their best bibbed over-alls, white shirts, and grey fedoras would crowd toward the outer stage to see an old, Clara Belle-type clown with an outrageous orange wig chat up the lust as he honked an old Tin Lizzie horn ("Ah-OOOOOGA!"), and brought out a "veteran" (is that a diplomatic way to describe an exotic artiste past her prime?) hootchie-cooch dancer, bare on top save for a couple of sparkling pasties with too-long tassles attached to each hidden nipple! Lowland farmers and hillbilly ridge-runners alike thought she was the epitome of forbidden fruit!

"Nah-nah-nah-nah-nah! Nah-nah-nah-nah-nah-nah-nah!

(Gimme that old Egyptian bump and grind!)

Nah-nah-nananananananana! (hips gyrating like a home-wrecker!) Nah-nah-nananananananana!

"Nah-nah-nah-nah-nah! Nah-nah-nah-nah-nah-nah-nah!

Dad told me how he and Uncle Woodrow got in trouble when they were little boys outside the Hootchie-Cooch Show back in their day. Dad and Wood were transfixed by the way the dancer's tassles whirled 'round and 'round, he said, both their little heads rotating in sympathy to her motion as the nasty old clown kept on saying something vaguely porno-graphic over and over, like "Rubber ball, rubber ball, rubber ball! (Rub her what?)," as he bounced an old red beach ball up and down. The boys were so mesmerized that they didn't hear Grandma and Grandpa step up behind them, catching them both with their hands in their pockets!

Grandma Sprinkle grabbed them each by the ear in righ-teous indignation, drawing them away from the pit of Hades yawning up under their horny little hides. Dad also remem-bered that she had to holler back for Grandpa to get out of there himself ("BANISTER! That means you, TOO!").

What is there about grotesques that draws us like moths

to a flame? Something that both attracts us and repels us at the same time? I remember reading columnist Leonard Pitts Jr.'s description of the open casket of slain African American teenager, Emmett Till, after his body had been fished out of the Tallahatchie River in 1955:

> *"The picture of him that was taken then, published in Jet magazine and flashed around the world, was stomach turning. A lively and prankish boy had become a bloated grotesquerie, an ear missing, an eye gouged out, a bullet hole in his head. You looked at that picture and you felt that here was the reason coffins have lids."*[1]

Joseph Carey Merrick (1862-1890), aka "The Elephant Man," a marvel of human deformity, refinement of mind, and sensitivity of soul, was reduced for a time to life as a sideshow grotesquerie. A letter to the Editor of The London Times summed up the experience of Mr. Merrick by the Chairman of the London Hospital:

> *"Terrible though his appearance is, so terrible indeed that women and nervous persons fly in terror from the sight of him, and that he is debarred from seeking to earn his livelihood in any ordinary way, yet he is superior in intelligence, can read and write, is quiet, gentle, not to say even refined in his mind."*[2]

I didn't have to slip into a carnival sideshow for my

---

[1] Leonard Pitts Jr., "Remembering a mother who devoted her life to keeping the casket open," Philadelphia Enquirer, January 11, 2003.

[2] F.C. Carr Gomm, "The Elephant Man," The Times, December 4, 1886, in The Dictionary of Victorian London: online: www.victorianlon-don.org/people/elephantman.htm. Accessed 5/24/2013.

grotesqueries, however. Country life among hard living folks without benefit of the best of health care provided me all I could stand, just by visiting Slaughter's Store, right across the White Dirt Road from Salem Fork Church where I belonged as a young member. Nobody there knew anything firsthand about plastic surgery. That was something reserved for Hollywood movie stars, not for Surry County dirt farmers. Even iodized salt was in short supply. I saw my first goiter at Slaughter's Store, big as twenty-pound raccoon, hanging off of a man's throat. God! I didn't know what it was, all purple and veiney, and couldn't keep myself from staring! Iodine deficiency causes the thyroid gland to swell, sometimes to a prodigious size, like the one I first saw at Slaughter's. The swelling made the man resemble the Star Wars villain, Jabba the Hut. As I remember it, though, he had a voice like a Wookie.

Then there was the man with a nose that would've made Jimmy Durante, "The Schnozz," jealous. I never knew his name, but he had a bulbous nose so long and fleshy that he had to move it out of the way with his hand just to drink a bottle of cold soda. I couldn't take my eyes off of him. He would push the slab of meat that was his nose out of the way with his thumb, turn up the bottle of Nehi Grape Soda he just bought, and swig away, as I watched him in fascination.

Of course, the grotesque is not limited to appearance. Perhaps the least common way grotesqueries are expressed is in how people look. More often, it is situational, or in what one does—a sideshow experience of how a person is in his or her essence. Mr. Jay Mack was like that. He was a denizen of Slaughter's Store, too. Jay made his living with a knife, castrating animals. Veterinarians were pretty thin on the ground in Surry County in those days. Either a farmer learned

Honeysucker

to castrate his own boar hogs and cattle, or he got a neighbor who specialized in "cuttin'" to do it for him. I know that this walks a fine line, but there was nothing vulgar about the way Jay lived and talked about his skills. There certainly was something grotesque about it, however.

Mr. Jay (or "Jaybird," as his associates called him, largely because of his birdlike, sing-song voice patterns), had a high-pitched laugh, darting eyes, jerky hand movements, and a shock of white hair. In his nasal whine, he delighted in holding a crowd spellbound around the pop crates at Slaugher's in the late afternoon, as the shadows lengthened—especially if there were little boys like me to mesmerize.

"I cut ever' thing from a rat to a cat! Yessir, cut ever' thing from a rat to a cat," he'd say, eyeing the crowd. "Gotta have a real sharp knife to do it, tho! Lookee h'year!" Mr. Jay would sing, whipping out his blade and shaving the hair off his forearm for a streak. "Sharp, ain't it, Boy?"

"Yessir, Mr. Jay," I'd say.

As he put up the knife, he waxed almost poetic. "Like I sed, I've cut ever' thing from a rat to a cat. Don't like to cut ol' tomcat though. Piss in yer face ever' time!"

"One time," he sang along, "I came up on a rabbit gum (a wooden rabbit trap, with a trip mechanism that closes swiftly behind an animal coming in to take the bait), and I knew for certain there's something in there! I picked up that ol' gum, opened the trap door, rammed my hand in there, and . . . pulled out a damned brown wood rat! Oooh-ee! Pulled him out by his tail, I did!"

68

"Well, I had my cuttin' knife, so just fer the hell of it, I pulled it out and cut him while I had his legs apart! I put ol' wood rat down and he ran wobblin' and bleedin' back into the woods, squealing, 'Wickity, wickity, wick!' Cleaned my cuttin' knife off and put it up. Y'see, I've cut ever' thing from a rat to a cat . . . Never have cut a man yet (and his voice dropped precipitously as he said it, looking in my direction). *Shore would like to, though!"* I nearly swallowed the jawbreaker I was working on, and took the next opportunity to hightail it on home!

Flannery O'Connor, the Georgia red clay short story writer of international renown, understood the instinctive attraction of Southerners for the grotesque. She wrote grotesque charac- ters into many of her most famous stories: an outlaw who went around the countryside exterminating families and comparing himself to Jesus; a reprobate grandfather who abandons his helpless grandson in alien Atlanta, only to seek redemption from a vandalized, iconic lawn ornament, a concrete jockey with half its face chopped off—"the Artificial N****r"; and a sadistic door-to-door Bible salesman who steals an ugly girl's wooden leg after making love to her in a hay loft. In her 1960 essay, "Some Aspects of the Grotesque in Southern Fiction,"[3] Ms. O'Connor explains why Southern writers deal with such harsh things. She writes:

> *"Whenever I'm asked why Southern writers particular- ly have a penchant for writing about freaks, I say it is because we are still able to recognize one. To be able to recognize a freak, you have to have some conception of*

3 Flannery O'Connor, "Some Aspects of the Grotesque in Southern Fiction," 1960. Online: www.en.utexas.edu/amlit/amlitprivate/scans/ grotesque.html. Accessed May 25, 2013.

the whole man, and in the South the general conception of man is still, in the main, theological."

Warming to her subject, she says:

"That is a large statement, and it is dangerous to make it, for almost anything you say about Southern belief can be denied in the next breath with equal propriety. But approaching the subject from the standpoint of the writer, I think it is safe to say that while the South is hardly Christ-centered, it is most certainly Christ-haunted. The Southerner, who isn't convinced of it, is very much afraid that he may have been formed in the image and likeness of God. Ghosts can be very fierce and instructive. They cast strange shadows, particularly in our literature."

Ms. O'Connor concludes her essay with crisp words about the freakishness of our visions and dreams:

"The novelist must be characterized not by his function but by his vision, and we must remember that his vision has to be transmitted and that the limitations and blind spots of his audience will very definitely affect the way he is able to show what he sees. This is another thing which in these times increases the tendency toward the grotesque in fiction."

Here endeth the lesson. Now, I ain't saying that I'm some sort of latter day Flannery O'Connor, but I have appreciated my share of freaks. And I suppose I see who I truly am a little bit better because of them.

Preachers and Money

Somehow, word got out to my grandmother and my great aunt that I was going to "make a preacher." I got summoned for questioning.

Grandma Sprinkle was a little bitty, snuff dipping mountain woman, a double predestinarian Primitive Baptist (not an oxymoron, by the way!). Double predestinarians believe that the fate of a person is sealed long before birth: that God "elects" or predestines people either for salvation in heaven, or damnation in hell. In the Southern Highlands, such believers are called "Hardshell Baptists." They meet for preaching once a month on Saturday evening ("the Sabbath"), wash feet annually in an age-old ritual of humility, argue endlessly about who can and who cannot preach at their services, and are universally reviled by Missionary Baptists. Opposition never seemed to faze them. It was all in God's plan. Countless times, I have heard Grandma say, "What is to be, will be; and what ain't to be, won't! The truth's the truth, and the truth will stand, even when the world's on fire!" I could smell the brimstone as she walked by. She loved me, no doubt; but she could be pretty grim.

Aunt Beulah was a Hardshell, too, but of the more mischievous variety. She lived up in Traphill, North Carolina, right at the foot of the mountains, where she farmed a little, and laughed a lot. Like Grandma, her sister, she dipped snuff and wore her hair in a bun on top of her head. But there the similarities stopped. Aunt Beulah was as wide as she was tall, and surrounded herself with animals for company: a big gray tom cat named "Whizzer" who got his name for whizzing in her cast iron sink, a huge black boar hog named "Brutus," and a dog so shaggy that you couldn't really tell which end was which until his tongue came flicking out. She called him "Dirty Dog."

Aunt Beulah called me "Little Boy" right up into my manhood. That was just her way. At the Inquisition, she did most of the talking.

"Little Boy! Little Boy! We heard tell you're called to preach among the Campbellites" (we attended the Disciples of Christ Church, called "Campbellites" by their detractors, after their most prominent frontier leader, Alexander Campbell). "Is that true? Are you called of the Lord to preach?"

I cleared my throat. Standing before two Hardshells like Grandma and Aunt Beulah was a mouth-drying experience. "Yes, Ma'am. I do think so," I said.

Aunt Beulah was on me like a hen on a june bug: "Think so? Think SO! There ain't no 'Think So'! There's only 'Is So,' or 'Is Not So'—which is it?"

I recanted and rephrased, immediately. "Yes, Ma'am. I understand, now. Yes, I am called to preach."

Aunt Beulah wrinkled up her nose at me, and shifted her snuff to another spot in her lip. "Well, then, I got another question for you, Little Boy! Are you called to preach for the Lord for money?"

"Why, Aunt Beulah?" I asked.

"Because, Little Boy!

Be-cause, if you preach for the Lord for money, you'll preach for the Devil for a raise!"

Man on the Moon

Did I ever tell you that my Grandma Sprinkle was a Hard-shell Primitive Baptist? Oh, she loved her grandchildren and had her soft side, for sure, but she was tough as a lighter knot (the choicest of the pine kindling, impossible to break up, but the best for starting a fire in the stove). I remember her coming around the corner of her little clapboard house, puffing and blowing because of her breathing problems: "Huff, puff! Huff, puff! Wh-e-e-e-e-z-e!" In response to any story of woe in the community, she would declare, "What is to be will be, and what ain't to be won't! The truth's the truth, and the truth will stand, even when the world's on fire!" Whoo-eee! You could smell the infernal sulphur brimming up around her!

"Hardshell" was in contradistinction to "Softshell." All Primitive Baptist believers were Calvinist; that is, they believed that God could tell what was going to happen before it did. And, both Hardshells and Softshells had the same practices: meeting for worship one Saturday a month, rather than on Sundays, and singing a capella, that is, totally without instrumental accompaniment. The big difference between the two sects was over how much of life on earth God foreordained and predetermined.

Now, the Softshells who met at Little Vine believed that the Sovereign God decided who was going to heaven, even before they did one faithful thing in their lives, or carried out a single good deed. These were the "Elect," and they lived out their lives in accordance with God's plan. But Softshells remained agnostic about who was going to hell. They were, in a word, Single Predestinarians.

Not Grandma's church, the Fisher River Mission. Hardshells were Double Predestinarian Primitive Baptists. They adhered to the rock-ribbed doctrine that the Sovereign God not only knew who was predestined for heaven. He also had determined who was going to hell, and there was nothing anybody could do about it. Elect for heaven or hell, before God had laid the very foundations of the world! Life was hard for farmers like Grandma's people, scrabbling out an existence in the rocky red dirt of the Blue Ridge Mountains, and Hardshell religion reflected the toughness of a lifestyle that made bears, catamounts, pine trees, and people tough enough to endure.

I looked forward to going over to Grandma's and Grandpa's house. It was a small boy's paradise. Grandma had little Rat Terriers, four or five at a time, and I loved running with them around the house, off the porch, and through the woodshed. She named all of them, "Trixie," 'cause she said it was just simpler that way. I guess she never could tell them apart. "Here, Trixie, Trixie!" she'd call, and they all yipped and yapped back to the house. They couldn't tell who was who, either.

Most of all, I loved it when Grandma called me into her sitting room to help her open the big chest of drawers where she kept her candy stash. Although she was a little woman, she was fully able to open the drawers by herself. She made me believe, like any good grandmother should, that she couldn't get to the candy without my help; so, she would take hold of one of the big brass handles, and I would grab onto the other, and we would p-u-u-u-u-l-l until the best candy you ever saw came into plain sight. Nobody had better candy than Grandma Sprinkle: peanut butter logs, chocolate drops, peppermint candy canes, and my favorite of them all, marshmallow circus peanuts—pastel orange colored, soft and sweet! We spent some pretty good times satisfying our sweet tooth together, in front of that big, open candy drawer.

For me to get the candy, though, I had to hear her out on her religion. You can endure a whole lot of things when the right candy is involved. For example, she didn't believe in Sunday School. She'd say, as we chewed on candy, "You cain't teach anybody religion. Religion cain't be taught. Either God gives it to ye, or ye don't get it at all. What is to be will be, and what ain't to be, won't . . . ," et cetera, et cetera, and so forth. I usually only half-listened through a sugar buzz.

I supposed I was made out of other religious stuff than that. Mama's folks, once Missionary Baptists, had become Disciples of Christ, also known as the "Campbellites." The

Campbellite influence gave me a love of learning, and, though I was mostly bored throughout high school, my summer at the Governor's School of North Carolina, held on the beautiful campus of Salem College down in Winston-Salem, opened doors and windows for me on the life of the mind that I didn't even know existed. I was a smart kid, and smart-assed, too. So, by the time I got to be a teenager, I was pretty sure I knew most everything.

 In the summer of my eighteenth year, 1969, freshly home from Governor's School and all that book learning, I came back to a community consumed with news of the Apollo 11 Moon Landing. You know, "One small step for a man, one giant leap for mankind," that moon landing, when Astronaut Neil Armstrong set foot on the lunar surface. Television was ablaze with reports of the moonwalk, televised from the surface of the moon.

Grandma wasn't having any of it! No, sir! It was all a hoax to her, and she had Hardshell religion to back her up. Standing amidst a bunch of family in her sitting room with the TV droning in the background, she began to pace.

"Ain't no such a thing! Ain't no such a thing!" she said in her shrill voice. "It never happened! I tell ye, they made the whole thing up! They all got together out there in Hollywood, and took a bunch of pictures like the ones they're a-showing on the TV. They're a-fooling everybody with 'em, I tell ye!"

Like a prosecutor to a jury, she brought her argument home:

"Why, if *Gawd* had a-wanted us to go walkin' around on the moon, we'd a-been born up there!"

My big mistake that day was standing too close to her when seized by a case of the smart-ass. "That's right, Grandma! That's right!" I said. "And if God had wanted us to run around naked all the time, we'd a-been born that way, too!"

I stood there grinning from ear to ear. My logic was unassailable. But my teeth weren't!

"Ker-Whap!" The next thing I knew, her knuckles were planted right smack up underneath my nose! Grandma had backhanded me with her fist, and she packed a wallop! She struck me lightning-fast like a black snake hitting a rat! Snot flew, and it was mine! I clapped both hands over my aching mouth, as she snapped, "Don't you back-sass me, boy! Don't you sass me!"

Amazed and dazed, I absorbed the lesson. You can truly be right, and dead wrong at the same time. If you're gonna contradict your Hardshell Baptist Grandma, at least have sense enough to do it out of fist range!

The Original Black Power

Grandma Sprinkle swore by patent medicine. The kind you bought at the general store, or out of a catalogue. That's how they did it up in the mountains of North Carolina: castor oil for the children, Wine of Cardui (38 proof) for "women's complaint," and Black Draught (pronounced, "Black Draft") for constipation.

Black Draught at Grandma's house came powdered in a little black and yellow box. You mixed a dose of it in warm water, applied it to the patient, and moved out of the line of fire. Grandma's primary patient was Grandpa. Grandpa Sprinkle ate bananas with abandon right off a big stalk that he got up at the store, even though they gummed up his works. "Per-naners back up on me, boy, but I love 'em so good," he would say. Grandma would dose him with Black Draught, and step back out of his way. Poor Grandpa had horrid arthritis, and he could only shuffle, even at top speed. He could barely get down his suspenders, and make it to the John. The Black Draught was so efficient, sometimes he didn't quite make it. More than once, I heard Grandma berating him all the way into the bathroom, "Banister, you have strowed yer sh*t all over the house like a mad woman!"

Purgatives were a standby for my grandparents' generation. A "purge" was good for what ailed you, and even celebrities and movie stars loved a good one. Louis "Satchmo" Armstrong and Elvis Presley were fabled devotees of "cathartics," as they were called. They say Elvis died on the can after a big one, you know. Others say he just left the building.

What gave Black Draught its impressive power was senna, dried leaflets of the Cassia acutiflora plant, crushed into a bitter-tasting granular powder, or brewed into a syrup. In the Blue Ridge Mountains, it was a cure-all. Headache? You needed to be cleaned out! Bowel problems? Getchya some in the palm of your hand, and lick it all gone. Melancholia? The Blues? Black Draught'll fix it!

Grandma could orate for hours on the virtues of Black Draught. She was a trip to talk with about anything, much less bowel problems. Her given name was Ila, and she was a teen-eintsy, pale skinned woman with a proud face full of hillbilly character. Like her sister, my Great Aunt Beulah, she wore her brunette hair pulled back and up, forming a bun secured by long, metal hairpins. Grandpa found and married her high in the North Carolina mountains, where she and her ancestors had lived for generations.

Grandma's people lived in an isolated area of the uplands where a nearly pure form of Elizabethan English survived, untroubled by modern speech and pronunciation. To listen to her talk was to travel back in time, to the 16th and 17th centuries in Shakespearean England. To the uninformed, her speech sounded strange and antique, maybe even ignorant. But Grandma Sprinkle spoke the nearly pure Elizabethan English of her mountain people, which had been correct three or four hundred years ago, and her way of talking delighted me.

"That yeller cat yonder clomb that gum tree yestiddy," she would say. "He clomb it slick as a whistle!" "Clomb," you see, was her way of making the verb "to climb" past tense. Instead of ending the verb with "–ed" to form the past tense, she had learned to lengthen the vowel.

"Brother Ransom (her small-framed blood brother) cum down h'year from up on the mountain, and holp me crop ter-baccer last week. Don't know what I'd-a done if'n he hadn't holpen me," she would say between dips of snuff.

Now, like I said, Grandma could orate on the gifts and graces of Black Draught with gusto. One hot summer afternoon on her porch, in the presence of my father, Thedford, Grandma embarrassed the hell out of him, and gave me something I could kid Dad about all day long.

I had never known anyone else named "Thedford" in my life, only my Dad.

So, I asked her as she rocked on her porch, "Grandma, how'd you come to name Dad the way you did?" She didn't miss a beat, pulling the little black and yellow box out of her apron pocket. She pointed to the words on the front label of the box: "Thedford's Black Draught."

Before Dad could stop her, she said, "When I was a-carrying yer Daddy (pregnant with him), I'se all bunged up terrible. I took me a dose-t of Black Draught, and it holp move me off! I'se so beholden to it, I named him for it!"

"Mama, shut up, I tell you!" Dad hollered. "The boy'll never let me live it down!"

I burst out in a face-cracking grin. "What? You named Dad for a laxative! Oh, my God! My Daddy is named 'Ex-Lax'! HAHAHAHAHAHA!"

Dad stomped off the porch and went out in the field to cool off. Grandma was tickled so much that she had to hold her sides. I'm pretty sure she enjoyed the moment every bit as much as I did. It's not every day a kid learns his Pop was named after the Original Black Power!

Apples on Clabber Mountain

In the pre-war years, Dad had a '38 Ford Roadster with a rumble seat—a thing of beauty to behold! It was a V8 Two-Door DeLuxe Convertible model, a rag top, as shiny black as a king snake, Dad said. He ran that Ford all over creation, looking all-outlaw like Clyde Barrow.

Grandma said she needed some good apples to make into pies, the kind that grew best in the high orchards. To her taste, lowland fruit was too sweet to make a good pie. She needed the tart kind, like those from up on the mountain. So, Dad, my Uncle Woodrow, and their best friends, the Cheney Brothers (Duke and Aubrey), told her to keep her money, and they tore off on the winding road up Clabber Mountain, nearly to the Virginia line to get her some apples. It was a recipe for trouble!

When they got up to where the orchards grew on top of the mountain, they stopped to haggle with the old man who had the best apples in the state (or so he said!). After they struck a deal on the apples, and had tied them in tow sacks to the rumble seat, the old mountain man said, "Boys, I got me some of the finest peach brandy ye ever tasted. How 'bout a little taste afore ye go on down the mountain?"

Well, they had some extra money burning a hole in their pockets, so they bought as many bottles of that peach brandy as they could carry. The Cheney Boys had a pen knife, so they just slipped it through the cork in the bottle, and their tongues got so happy they near 'bout slapped out their back teeth, that brandy was so good! Smooth as silk, and pure-tee de-licious!

Now, to appreciate the rest of the story, you need to know something about brandy. Brandy is a fortified or distilled wine, made from grapes and grape hulls (called "pomace"), or from a variety of other fruits, in this case, peaches. Peach brandy, like the sort the old mountain man sold the Sprinkle and Cheney Brothers, did not require aging before it was bottled. The product was clear-looking as spring water, 40% to 45% alcohol by volume (80 to 90 U.S. proof); and though it might taste as sweet as a pie, it packed a hell of a wallop Dad and the other boys didn't count on. How they ever got down that mountain in one piece, none of them ever knew, but it was party time in that '38 Roadster! Those boys strewed apples all over Clabber Mountain! They did everything but flip the car, I guess, and by the time they got back to Grandma's and Grandpa's, they were all as drunk as stewed owls, and the only apples left were a couple that got twisted up in the only tow sack they didn't lose over the side of the mountain. Grandma was not pleased.

The weekdays passed so slowly, and whenever Dad, Wood, and the Cheney Boys saw each other after work in the tobacco fields, all they could talk about was that elixir of the gods, the old man's peach brandy. It was so smooth that none of them got even a slight hangover, no matter how stumble-down drunk they had been. For sure, they resolved to get them some more of that fine peach brandy as soon as they could!

So, the next weekend, galvanized by Grandma's rock ribbed admonition that she was gonna have her some good apples from up yonder, OR ELSE, Dad, Woodrow, Duke, and Aubrey took off on the long climb up Clabber Mountain in Dad's Roadster.

A word about Western North Carolina directions seems in order. Grandma said she was gonna get her some apples from "up yonder" or know the reason why. "Yonder" is a distance term with rather precise meanings for those in the know (don'tcha know!).

- "Yonder" is the equivalent of "over there in the near distance."
- "Over yonder" means "a little further over there" in mountain speak.
- "Up yonder" refers, in this case, to the relentlessly inclining road up the mountain, as in "I'm a' gonna go up yonder today and get me summa them damned apples!"
- "Way up yonder" means "climb till the air gets chilly and a little too thin for a flat lander to breathe without huffing and puffing."
- "Way up in yonder" or "way back up in yonder" is a more-or-less specific direction and distance combo leading to the old mountain man's apple orchard atop Clabber Mountain, and then down a secluded one-lane dirt road to his cabin in the woods.

Got it yet, Yankee?

Well, they made it way up back in yonder to the old mountain man's cabin, and bought as many apples as they could bag and cram in the rumble seat. There was no way they were going to face Grandma Sprinkle again without producing the apples she demanded over a week ago. Feeling pretty secure this time, Dad asked if he could get him a taste of some of that marvelous peach brandy again.

"Naw," the old man allowed. "Last time you boys drunk up all a' that I had left. But foller me," he said, taking off around the rickety corncrib. "I'll show ye what I do have!"

There, arranged like soldiers in ranks, were row upon row of sawhorses topped with wooden planks to make shelves, sitting in the shade of the apple trees. A grape arbor stood off to the side, an old one, laden with purple grapes on some vines, and white ones on the others. It was high Indian summer, and the yellow jackets, wasps, bald-faced hornets, and honeybees were making the best of it, swarming over the ripening fruit. Stacked upright with military precision atop those shelves were long necked green glass bottles filled with new grape wine (spo-dee-o-dee!)! The bottles had no corks, but instead were capped with the same metal lids soda bottles had, often called "crown caps" because of the way the lid was crimped around the edges to achieve the seal. Very well. But the wine was obviously still "green," Dad said, and it looked evil to him, bubbling and working in the necks of those bottles like witches' brew. It was still fermenting in the bottles like crazy.

Since green wine was all the old mountain man had to sell the thirsty young men, they bought a couple of crates, wedged their bodies in among the apples, cranked up the Roadster, and they were off down the mountain. Because they didn't have a churchkey (bottle opener), they had to use their pocket knives to pry off the lids.

The still-fermenting wine had so much pressure trapped in those green long-necked bottles that when the Cheney Boys snapped off the cap with their knives, all the contents shot out with a rush of volcanic energy, soaking themselves, Dad and Woodrow! One after another, those bottles shot their wad all over the car, down into the floorboards, and over the side of the mountain like a series of mini geysers! Dad struggled to keep the car between the side ditches, as Duke and Aubrey cussed those bottles and failed to get themselves even a mouthful of it!

Aubrey had a temper—everybody in Salem Fork knew it—a bad temper that sometimes clouded his judgment and pushed him to do things he later regretted. This was such a moment. He let out an oath that would make a preacher blush!

"Hot damn, Thedford, BY GAWD, I'm gonna get me some of that G-D wine if'n it's the last thing I ever do!" And in one deft motion, Aubrey popped the lid off a bottle with the flat of his knife, and jammed the whole neck of the thing into his mouth and part way down his throat! Dad, watching it all in the rear view mirror while steering for the center of the road, saw it all! Aubrey's eyes bugged out like goose eggs! That wine exploded into Aubrey's mouth so hard that it had to escape somewhere—and two long columns of foaming, still-fermenting wine flew streaming out of Aubrey's nose holes like the exhaust water powering a jet ski! It hit Woodrow on the back of his bald head, and blew his brand new Panama hat out of the car! Duke was laughing at his brother so hard he didn't even help the poor man who was strangling and gagging on the residue of the wine that had near 'bout dislodged his ad-enoids out his nose! Dad pulled the car to a stop, and yanked on the hand brake.

Laughing so hard he almost coughed up a lung himself, Duke jumped out of the back seat, and taunted his brother, "HAHAHAHAHA! Gotche some wine that time, didn't ye, ol' boy!"

Aubrey lept out on his side, balled up one of his fists, and gripped the empty wine bottle in the other, brandishing it over his head like a belaying pin. "BY GAWD, I'm a' DYIN' over here! That damned wine's a' burnin' me up alive, and all you can do is LAUGH at me like a damned JACKASS! Why, I'll knock ye into next week when I catch ye!"

The Cheney Boys, deranged with laughter and covered in green, wicked wine, rushed headlong into a blackberry briar patch. Duke nearly tore off his britches, and Aubrey looked like he caught a wildcat barehanded, and got the worse end of the deal. Woodrow and Dad had to climb after them into that thicket full of briars to pull them out.

Broke, soaked, and scratched all to hell, they finally rolled into the Sprinkle home place. Grandma finally got her ap-ples to make her pies, even if the Sprinkle Brothers and the Cheney Boys, much to their chagrin, never did get themselves a mouthful of that wicked, wicked wine (spo-dee-o-dee!)!

Stealing Grandpa's Tractor

Grandpa Sprinkle was in a sad state after Grandma died. Truth is, he went a bit crazy from the grief. The winter following her death was severe. The only heat in the house was from an old-style Ziegler Oil Heater that stood in Grandpa's combination living room and bedroom. His pernicious arthritis got so bad that he couldn't turn the knob to increase the oil flow, and when we visited him, the house was as cold as a freezer locker. Dad and I found him shivering in front of the little open hatch of the heater, false teeth chattering, with his tormented hands cupped around the little blue pilot light.

After we got him into bed and fixed the heater, Grandpa got much worse. He lay in the bed calling out Grandma's name, claiming that he could see her clothed in a white gown, floating around in the air with no legs. At one moment he would berate her for every imagined slight he could think of, and the next he would cry pitifully for her to return to him. "Ila! Ila! Won'tcha come home to me?" he would moan.

A hospital wouldn't do him much good, the doctor said. "Better to keep him in a familiar place, at home, if you can." So, Dad and his brothers, my Uncle Woodrow, and my Uncle Culbert, had a meeting, and decided to take shifts staying with Grandpa until he got better, or worse. Every third night after work, Dad and I would go out to Grandpa's house to relieve Culbert and his wife, Stella. The room was warm enough, but dimly lit and ethereal. Dad sat in Grandma's swan necked rocking chair, and promptly went to sleep, snoring steadily. I sat beside him on the couch beneath the porch window. The only sound other than Dad's snoring, and the tick-tock-tick of Grandma's mantle clock, was the muttering of my increasingly delusional Grandpa.

That clock deserves separate mention. It was a large, bronze colored clock, depicting President Franklin Delano Roosevelt standing with his sure hands on the wheel of the ship of state. The ship's wheel encompassed the clock face. FDR, whom Grandma and Grandpa idolized, stood upright, looking confidently into the future, seeming to reassure everyone that "The only thing we have to fea-ah is fea-ah itself." At the time the clock was manufactured, few members of the public knew the President had crippling polio, and could not stand without leg braces. That mantle clock perpetuated the hope of the New Deal, a testimonial that "Happy Days Are Here Again!" I have no idea what happened to that marvelous clock. I wish I did.

Grandpa couldn't walk any more. He had to use a bedpan to relieve himself, and we had to clean him up. Such is the human condition. He lay in the bed, refusing to go to sleep in the muddle of his mind. But he was still strong, and he could move surprisingly quickly when some interior demon goaded him to try and jump out of the bed. Since Dad slept so soundly and I slept so lightly, my job was to hear Grandpa start to spring out of bed. I would lunge off the couch and kick Dad in the shin to wake him up in the same motion. Calling out would have done no good—not when Dad was sound asleep. Dad, aroused from his deep sleep, would automatically throw himself forward, and it often took both of us to pin Grandpa down in order to keep him from falling headlong onto the floor.

One freezing, bleak midwinter night, Grandpa was muttering to himself in the bed. By turns, he would berate Grandma for leaving him alone, preach like a Primitive Baptist preacher (for in later life, he had converted to Grandma's church—one of the few cases of a Missionary Baptist going over to the Hardshells I had ever heard of), and then pick imaginary worms off of his hands and arms. Grandpa had just thought he saw my Uncle Woodrow trying to climb into the sitting room window from outside. "Wood!" Grandpa said, "Get down outta that winder . . . ye know yer too fat to get in here thataway!" I could barely hold back my laughter. Then Grandpa went back to plucking off his imaginary worms.

In the midst of the mumbling, the Unthinkable happened! There is no delicate way to put this. Dad had gas, bad gas! He could float an air biscuit in a skinny minute, even in his sleep! Though he never heard a thing, Dad let the biggest fart rip that night I had ever heard in my teenage life! The sound split the silence in two, like the rending of the veil of the Temple, from top to bottom:

"Bar-r-r-r-r-r-a-a-a-a-p-p-p-p!" Then, "Bar-r-r-r-r-r-a-a-a-a-p-p-p-p! Bar-r-r-r-r-r-a-a-a-a-p-p-p-p!" again! It was a three-staged, turbo-charged blutter-blaster—the kind that would've knocked the Stetson hat off a Texas Congressman! I swear that fart took a whole 20 seconds to explode out into the open!

In astonishment, I saw my poor, crazy old Grandpa sit right straight up in the bed and holler out, "Woodrow, son, hurry up! Somebody's cranked up the tractor and is stealin' it outta the shed! I hear its motor a-roarin'!"

Grandpa was right! That's exactly what it sounded like! I laughed so hard that it woke Dad up, dazed and confused. "What the hell's goin' on?" he demanded. So, I told him!

"HAHAHAHAHAHA! You just farted SO loud you made Grandpa think somebody had cranked up the tractor and was stealing it!" I gasped! "HAHAHAHAHA!" I was wiping tears from my eyes, I laughed so hard!

Dad was as defensive as a wompus cat with a sore paw (a wompus cat is a black one with a cherry red bum hole). "Quit makin' sh*t up!" he hollered. "I never did such a thing!" Then, since Grandpa had quieted down, Dad settled back into the rocking chair, and commenced snoring again, as if nothing ever happened.

Of course, the whole thing was prophesied in the Good Book, Exodus 19:19:

"As the blast of the trumpet grew louder and louder, Moses would speak, and God would answer him in thunder."

Nay, I say! Forsooth and nay! Be gone! Ne'er speak thus again, thou toothless wonder!

All Day Preachin'
and Dinner on the Grounds

Homecoming was the biggest event of the year in Salem Fork. I'm not talking about homecoming at the high school, though that was fun, too. Naw. I'm talking about Church Homecoming: all day preachin' and dinner on the grounds. For one thing, it was the one time when everybody was not only welcome at church, but everybody was expected to be there, too.

Homecoming at Salem Fork was a showcase for the preacher, the choir, and for food, food, glorious FOOD! Our church was served through the years by three generations of preachers from the same family: Rev. Rufus Cooley, Rev. Grady Cooley (his son), and Rev. H.G. Cooley (Ol' Man Rufus's grandson). All three came over the mountains from Galax, Virginia to hold services and preach at our church on Fourth Sunday. We were a quarter-time church.

One Sunday out of each month, then, we had preaching. But Sunday School and Church were held each Sunday, without fail, even in snowy weather. Our Choir, none of whom could read music but the pianist, Cousin Doris Gabbard, led the singing and sometimes treated God to an anthem. Mama and my Aunt Irene both sang in the Choir. Mama sang alto, and Irene sang bass—yep, that's correct, bass, right along with Mr. Joe Long and Mr. Bernard Toon. Laugh all you want to, but Irene had what Cousin Doris called "perfect pitch." She could "heist" ("hoist" in Salem Fork Speak) the tune first time, every time, dead on the money!

The elders of the congregation divided up responsibilities, and led the service on the first three Sundays of each month. For example, Mr. Leroy Snow would preside at the Sunday School assembly and give the Opening Prayer ("Oh, Gawd, we're mighty glad to be h'yere . . . ."). Mr. Grover Simmons would read the Bible lesson for the Church service. My Uncle Ray and Mr. Rufus Shinault would preside at the Communion Table—a feature of Sunday worship that was always carried out, come hell or high water. But preaching was reserved for the Fourth Sunday of the month, when one of the Cooleys crossed the mountains and came down to "rightly divide the Word of truth" for the saints (and bad sinner boys like me).

Communion was special for us children because of my Grandma Bessie. Bessie made the communion bread for church every week for forty years. None of these store bought "chicken pellets" for the saints at Salem Fork! Oh, no! Not as long as Bessie Martin had anything to say about it. She baked unleavened bread (bread with no yeast in it) in the oven of her wood stove every weekend of the world. How she did it, I will never know. How did she manage to regulate the heat in a wood burning stove, and not char the daylights out of that delicate loaf of flat bread she hand rolled out so meticulously with her rolling pin? Bessie took a blunt old kitchen knife and softly scored the top of the dough just enough so it came out of the oven lightly browned and seemed to have the texture of the back of your hand—after all, this was the Body of Christ, right?

Bessie also prepared the grape juice for each service, too. One-by-one, she filled up those tiny little individual glasses (I called them "shot glasses" to make Communion more interesting) with the sweet fruit of the vine. We children were tantalized by those itty-bitty glasses of violet nectar, drawn to them like bear cubs to honey. But, of course, since we were too little to be baptized, we couldn't partake of the communion as it was passed down the pews in aluminum trays. That's where Bessie took over for our sakes. After church, she had the job of getting up all the cups and trays to take them home and wash them out for next week.

She would gather all the children around the Communion Table with a stage whisper, as if what was about to happen was our little secret, and ours alone. Then she would open up the lids of the communion trays, and the aroma of sweet grape juice would blossom and fill the room! With a solemn little smile on her face, Bessie would offer the tiny unused cups of juice to us, and say, "Now, you can have all you want of this till it's every bit gone! We don't need to tell anybody else about this, do we? Let's just keep it amongst us, okay?" No bunch of little children were ever more grateful to get a small taste of grape juice. Forbidden fruit is always the sweetest. Bessie would urge us on, making each one of us feel oh-so-special. "Go ahead and drink it up, y'hear, 'cause I surely don't need to take any of it home. Y'know, I think you're all mighty cute kids." Every child at Salem Fork was her grandchild around that Communion Table.

For Homecoming, we Campbellites pulled out all the stops! It was a big day, with former members and folks from all over the community coming back to the old home church. The blond oak pews in the sanctuary were jam-sandwich-full, people dressed in their very best, shoulder-to-shoulder, with chairs set up in the center aisle (that's how you knew it was a good Sunday—if chairs were set up in the aisle). Preacher Cooley (whichever one it happened to be that year) would give a surprisingly calm and well-reasoned message. Campbellites were known for that style of preaching, not the Baptist type, all white with foam. Nobody shouted during a Campbellite service, either.

Ol' Man Rufus Cooley was once famously challenged about the outwardly emotionless character of worship at Salem Fork. A Shouting Methodist, known for whoopin' out "A-may-yen!" multiple times when her preacher preached, cornered Mr. Rufus one day and demanded:

"How come y'all don't shout to the Lord during service? You oughta cry Holy to the Lord! Don'tcha believe in anything strong enough to shout about it?"

Unperturbed, Mr. Rufus replied, "Oh, shoutin's fine, . . . if you can't help it. But if you can help it, and you go ahead and shout anyway, why, you're just puttin' on!" Then he delivered the *coup de grâce* to his flabbergasted Methodist whooper. "And another thing, Sister. It's fine to holler and whoop all you want during church on Sunday, but don't go cheatin' your neighbor in a cow trade on Monday!"

Those Cooleys were smart men. All three of them were school teachers up in Galax, and Mr. Grady Cooley was a school principal. They read books. They knew something, I'll tell ye!

Just before the last hymn, the women would excuse themselves in droves to set out the Dinner on the Grounds. The men had already set up tables on the freshly trimmed church lawn, stretching the full length of the building. Oh, My Gawd! Such food you have never seen in your life! Fried chicken, roast beef, country ham biscuits and red-eye gravy, salty fat back meat, luscious barbecue, and potatoes—sliced, mashed, au gratin, and seasoned up every which a way! Fresh sweet corn, collard greens, turnips, macaroni and cheese, and mysterious casseroles that hid their ingredients but were delicious anyway! Pickled beets, pickled okra, pickled crab apples and spiced peaches, watermelon rind pickles, and 21-day pickles, prepared to perfection in a stoneware crock! And, whoo-eee, the desserts! The pies—pecan, blackberry, dutch apple, banana cream, and coconut cream topped with golden meringue as high as Carl Martin's mama's hair, in the upright and locked position! The fresh coconut cake, white as a wedding dress and sweet as a first kiss! Gluttony was taken off the list of the Seven Deadlies on Homecoming Sunday, 'cause everybody was expected to gorge themselves silly that day!

The one person you absolutely did not want to get behind in the food line was Raymond. If you did, you'd starve. I never saw a human being eat as much as that man could. He went down the tables like a Hoover vacuum cleaner, sucking up every crumb. Bald headed Raymond had a deep baritone voice and a set of store bought teeth he was mighty proud of. He'd tell you how he suffered from "Dunlop's disease" if you'd give in and listen to the same joke he'd told everybody about ten times already: "Boys, my belly's done lopped over my belt! H'yeh, h'yeh, yeh!"

One Homecoming, Raymond bragged up a storm about how much he could eat. "Boys, I'll tell ye," he said. "You can eat a pone a' cornbread, eat a pound a' hot dawgs, eat a pot full a' pinto beans, drink a quart of buttermilk, and when ye lay down in bed at night (he threw his hands up over his head for effect), yore legs'll stick right straight up toward the ceiling, and ye cain't put 'em down!"

I bet that was right . . . and I also bet he stirred up such a wind that he couldn't keep the sheets on the bed, either!

$5 and a Bushel of Corn

"Stick 'em under 'til they bubble!" That's how the Campbellites (otherwise known as the Disciples) at Salem Fork baptized converts. Everybody else for miles around was a Baptist of some flavor or other. There were more Baptists in our neck of the woods than there were people. I used to think that even the dogs and cats were Baptist—they fought like they were, anyway.

Salem Fork, four miles outside Dobson, the county seat, had two little churches and one little country store. There were the Missionary Baptists, the Campbellites where Mama's people were members, and the country store that belonged to my Cousin Gladys, Uncle Coot's eldest daughter. Gladys's Store had more members than both churches put together. It was a favorite of the men in the community.

At Gladys's Store, the men congregated to gossip and get themselves a cold drink in the afternoons. Don't ever let anybody tell you that women are the biggest gossips—men beat women at gossiping hands down! They liked to sit in a circle around the wood stove on Gladys's ladder back chairs, smoke cigars, drink a cold pop (or something stronger if they could smuggle it in), and talk big. Real big.

Out of the earshot of their wives, the men would go down the list of the world's troubles, and solve them all, one-by-one. First, they would "straighten out" their women. Then, they took on politics and whatever community indiscretion was making the gossip circuit. Finally, they would turn their attention to religion.

One time I saw my little bitty Great Uncle Ransom quarrel with Grandpa Sprinkle over who was right, the Primitive Baptists or the Missionary Baptists. Uncle Ransom was so short, he had to get up in the backend of a pickup truck to argue eye-to-eye with Grandpa. The old men whooped and hollered at each other like monkeys on moonshine, and Uncle Ransom popped his fist into the flat of his hand until his palm turned blue. In the end, they called it a draw, and went back into Gladys's to get a drink. That was usually the way arguments over religion ended up.

When the Campbellites up at Salem Fork had a revival, however, the arguments could almost get overwrought. Revivals were when out-of-town evangelists, the big guns, preached for converts, after which baptisms would occur where all the local churches baptized: at a lovely location on Mitchell's River owned by Mr. Willie Byrd. The churches kept the site down below the Mountain Park Bridge clear and clean in return for the gratis use of the spot to immerse the new members of the various churches. The water at Willie Byrd's was perfect: pristine, clear as a whistle, and so very chilly, even in the summertime. Mitchell's River flowed straight down the slope of Fisher's Peak in the Blue Ridge Mountains and wound its way through Willie Byrd's property to fulfill the needs of the saints.

But if every church in the community agreed to use the same spot on the river to baptize, that didn't mean they agreed on much of anything else. Baptists couldn't sit horses, so to speak, with the way the Campbellites at Salem Fork believed salvation came to the soul. For Baptists, what mattered was a sorrowful confession of faith accompanied by repentance. The Campbellites did, too, but they went one step further—contending that the Good Book mandated that their converts be immersed or plunged "in living water" (running water, like at Willie Byrd's) to seal the deal. The Baptists immersed their converts, as well, but they didn't hold to baptism as an absolute necessity like the Campbellites did. The Baptists mocked the Campbellites mercilessly for preaching the "water gospel" because of the importance water baptism held for them. Now, is that clear as mud to you yet, Dear Reader?

So, when Preacher Cooley and his visiting evangelist, the Rev. Mr. Coffee (yep, his real name), announced that the 14 converts won over at the Salem Fork Campbellite Revival were to be baptized Saturday at Willie Byrd's, the men at Gladys's Store argued religion like bishops fighting over an offering plate. The opening volley came from a member of the Baptist persuasion:

"Them Campbellites don't believe in Jesus!" he exclaimed. "They believe the water'll save ye. They preach the 'water gospel'! Why, I don't believe they even ask a feller for a confession of faith! They just stick 'em under without one! They just jump into that water a dry devil, and come up a wet devil!"

A staunch member of the Campbellite party answered:

"That ain't so! I know it ain't! My wife's cousin is one of them Campbellite elders, and they're as good a people as you! I believe they do ask for a confession of faith before they dunk ye!"

It was on then!

"Do not!"

"Do so!"

"Do not!"

"Do so!"

Then money started to fly. "John the Baptist" threw down a bill on top of the cracker barrel. "I'll bet you five dollars the Campbellites don't ask for a confession of faith before they baptize you!"

The second five-dollar bill hit the barrelhead. "Alexander Campbell" said, "I'll take that bet, 'cause I know they do!"

The money grew to a pile, everybody choosing a side! But nobody there expected it would cost anybody anything, since there was no way to secure the bet, and prove things one way or another. Then, one of the men looked over at a young man leaning on a stack of pop crates near the back door of the store. This boy, a late blooming teenager, had the reputation of being a bit slow in school. Some said he was about one sandwich shy of a full picnic basket. In that less kind age, he was referred to as "addle-pated."

So, the men drew the youth into their circle, and before you knew it, he had agreed to go down to Willie Byrd's on baptizing day, get in the back of the line, and pretend to be one of the converts for a bribe of five dollars and a bushel of corn—just to see once and for all if the Campbellites would baptize him without a confession of faith or not!

Sure enough, on baptizing day, instead of 14 converts, there were 15 standing in the line, ready to go down into the water to be baptized. The "addle-pated" boy was right there, almost counting his money and his corn, with a grin on his face. He was dressed just right, too, with a white shirt and dark pants, like the rest of the men to be baptized, and he even had a handkerchief in his hand to give to the preachers to clap over his nose so water wouldn't choke him when they dunked him under backwards, as the Campbellites practiced the rite.

To cover his bet, however, the main Campbellite sympathizer from Gladys's Store also showed up. He spoke with his wife's cousin, the elder, and a moment later the elder waded out into the water to speak to Mr. Cooley and Mr. Coffee.

"There's a young man here today to make a mockery of us," the elder said. "See him up there at the end of the line? He's been bribed for five dollars and a bushel of corn to prove we don't ask for a confession of faith before we baptize!" Then, with a solemn wrinkle in his brow, the elder asked, "Shall the elders and I eject him?"

Preacher Cooley looked toward Mr. Coffee and then said in reply, "Naw. No need of that. Just let me handle it."

Baptisms in the river moved along sort of like a holy assembly line. The preacher would receive the convert about thigh deep in the water, put one of his hands in the small of the convert's back, and ask if the convert indeed believed in Jesus Christ (See! Told ye so!). Upon his confession, the preacher would raise his other hand over the confessor, and announce, "Upon your profession of faith, I baptize you in the name of the Father, and the Son, and the Holy Ghost!" and in one smooth movement take the handkerchief provided, plant it firmly over the nose and mouth of the person, and swiftly dunk him backwards in the water. While the other preacher received the newly baptized believer and helped him back toward the riverbank, the next subject stepped up, and the process began rapid-fire all over again.

Preacher Cooley had a good rhythm going. He baptized 12, then 13, then 14, . . . and then he took hold of the boy who had been bribed up at Cousin Gladys's Store. Mr. Cooley looked him straight in the eye, clapped the handkerchief over his mouth, and plunged him under the water, saying in his loudest, clearest preacher voice, "In the Name of Five Dollars and a Bushel of Corn, I'll Send You To Hell As Sure As You're Born!"

That poor boy popped up spouting like a whale, broke loose from Preacher Cooley, fairly ran across the top of the water to scramble up the bank, and raced up the Mountain Park Road hollering, "M'God! M'God! That ol' preacher tried to drown me!"

The last the saints saw of him that day was as he tore outta there like his tail was on fire and his head was a-catching, his shirttail flapping out behind of his britches like a white flag of surrender! It was a true Shirt-tail Skedaddle!

There was no joy in Baptist-ville that day, I can tell ye!

Tastes Like Peppermint Candy

Each of Mama's sisters provided me with something I needed, something only each particular aunt could deliver. Irene, the eldest of the sisters, was wise. When I needed wisdom, I went to Aunt Irene. Lora was bossy. When I needed bossing around, and had to be told off, Aunt Lora filled the bill to a tee. But when I needed cheering up (which was often, for losing my mother to cancer at an early age had made a morose boy out of me), I went looking for my Aunt Joyce. Joyce could always make me laugh out loud.

Bessie, my grandmother, had studio photos of Joyce as a teenager, sepia-toned and glamorous—an extravagance for a small-time farm family. Bessie must have saved up her egg money for a long time to scrape together enough to have a professional photographer take Joyce's portrait photos. But that was a sacrifice a mother would make for a baby daughter of such rare beauty. Joyce had been ravishingly attractive as

111

a young woman—movie star beautiful, some said. On rainy afternoons when confined to Bessie's house, I would shuffle through Joyce's World War II vintage glamour shots, and marvel at how gorgeous she was. Even in matronly middle age, she retained the echoes of her youthful good looks: high cheek bones, perfectly proportioned facial features, and a gorgeous smile. It was a no-brainer why Uncle Art, a handsome Army Air Corps officer from far-off Michigan, relentlessly courted her, put a ring on her finger, and then bundled her away to Yankeeland at the close of the Good War. Like so many young couples thrown together by the fortunes of war, North Carolina Joyce and Michigan Art had met in Baltimore where she worked at a defense industry plant fabricating fighter planes to defeat the Nazis.

Joyce and Art made their home in western, small town Michigan, close by Art's dad and mom, and reared my two first cousins, Susan and Jane, there. Art had grown up on a farm, too—dairy cows, field crops, potatoes, and blueberries—so our family could relate to him readily. After the war, he used his G.I. Bill to attend Michigan State University, home of the Spartans. He became a County Agricultural Extension Agent, a veritable "Hank Kimball," the fictional, comic county agent in the hit television series, Green Acres. When Uncle Art let me make his rounds with him to visit the farms of Barry County, I used to hum the Vic Mizzy theme from Green Acres to myself, an homage to Eva Gabor: "Dah-ling I love you but give me Park Avenue!"

Joyce, as the county agent's wife, always made a command appearance at the closing banquet of the annual Barry County Fair, held in mid-July. The agricultural fair was the biggest event of the year, and families from all over western Michigan

112

came to show their livestock, cheer the harness racers, experience the carnival midway with its sideshows and rides, get their huge, mutant vegetables judged, and win a year's worth of bragging rights for the best pie in the county. The Banquet was the climax of the fair, and the Barry County Ag Agent and his family (I was snuck in with Suze and Jane, since nephews didn't normally qualify) had seats of honor in the Pavilion where the weight of kitchen delicacies made the tables moan.

Berry pies topped off lunch, glorious, architectural creations filled with secret ingredients passed down by generations of Swedish, German, and Dutch immigrant women to secure the coveted Blue Ribbon. If the ladies had needed to hot-oil wrestle each other to take the prize home, they surely would have, but this battlefield was dominated only by pie.

Joyce was a tasting judge by marriage, you might say. Pie cooks were eager to please her. So, I thought nothing of it when she was presented with a wedge of whole strawberry pie, topped with a Pike's Peak of whipping cream. She shoveled a mouthful in greedily. Later, in the aftermath of her near brush with Valhalla, she told me that the pie had a strange texture to it. She said she couldn't quite make out what the secret ingredient was. Besides the strawberries, there was Something Else. She rolled it around with her tongue. It was firm, she said, sort of tubular and round, like macaroni. She bit down on it, and it tasted just like peppermint candy! How odd! She lifted her fork, and discretely spit out the unswallowed portion so she could look at it.

The elderly lady sitting across the table from her said, "Are you alright, *meine Liebe* ("my dear")? You look pale, like you've seen a ghost!"

Joyce couldn't say anything, 'cause the sight of the secret ingredient froze her in place. All she could do was grasp her throat with her free hand. She opened her mouth, but no sound came out.

Her elderly tablemate saved her the trouble: *"Mein Gott in Himmel!"* the old lady shrieked! "She bit the tail off a *GRUB VÖRM!"* Then, she whooped out something else unintelligible in German, as if she had bitten down on the worm herself, and not Aunt Joyce. Then, *"Dere vas a GRUB VÖRM, im der Erdbeeren Kuchen, in der schtrawberry pie!"*

Pandemonium! Chaos! Apocalypse! Here comes the comet! Head for the hills, the dam's done busted! All hell broke loose in the kitchen!

Joyce sat in the wooden folding chair, gagging, with her eyes bugging out. There on the edge of her plate lay the monster with its little chubby tail nipped off.

A gastric heave or two, a couple of glasses of water, and Joyce managed to get most of her color back. The chef came out bowing and apologizing profusely to her, begging her pardon! How could such a thing have happened!?!

So, in order to save face and make up for this gustatory insult, the chef presented her . . . a fresh slice of . . . (ulp!) . . . *strawberry pie.*

Petticoat Preacher

As a boy of 15, I received "the call" to preach—an itching you cannot scratch without serving the church. But I should not have been the first in my family, not by a long shot. By default only, I became the first family divine. Had the door to ordained ministry not been shut tight to women because of social convention and backslidden theology, the first should have been my Aunt Irene White.

Aunt Irene, the eldest and wisest of my mother's siblings, had the sensibilities of ministry—what mountain folk called "the makin's of a preacher." Irene lived out her days as a deaconess and choir member at Salem Fork Christian Church, but she could expound upon the goodness of God with any male minister—and make more good sense than the lot of 'em! She was at the church any time the doors cracked open, and she loved it. "Oh, how I love the brethren," she used to say (I am sure she meant "the sistren," too, but that was just the way Christians of her vintage talked).

A dyed-in-the-wool Campbellite, she and Mama had a snappy comeback for anyone foolish enough to criticize their beloved church. "Better to be a Campbellite than no light at all!" they'd say as they verbally blew away a Baptist. Irene had a fine mind, well tuned by decades of voracious reading. One of my favorite tableaux of her was as she sat reading a book after a long day of farming and cooking for farmhands, resting in the waning sunshine that came through her kitchen window, smoking Kool Menthols. She had studied French, and loved to parlez-vous on the porch swing in the cool of the evening. Like her sisters Lora and Joyce, she had gone to far off Maryland to work in the World War II Defense Industry, building fighter planes for Uncle Sam. After the war, when my Uncle Paul returned from the Pacific where he fought on Guadalcanal, she returned with him to the small tobacco farm that sustained them, and they had a son, Philip, whom I called "Whitey" because of his pale blond hair.

Irene loved to tell about the founding days of the Salem

Fork Church, stories she heard from her mother, Bessie, from Grandma Dell, and from Uncle John, her father's loquacious brother. She could recount all the names of the preachers at Salem Fork since the beginning, and talk about the best points of each one, especially Mr. Hoffman, Mr. Taylor, and the three generations of Cooleys who came over the mountains from Coal Creek, Virginia to preach on fourth Sundays. But Irene loved nothing better than to tell Campbellite victory stories— tales of how her elders had bested their theological opponents, either through guile or superior intellect.

Her favorite tale was about Minnie Ruth, whose daddy was Head Deacon up at Salem Fork Baptist Church. As a teenager, Miss Minnie had come down to revival meetings at the Christian Church, and had been persuaded to make her confession of faith amongst the Campbellites—a scandal! Revivals were a twice-a-year phenomenon in the North Carolina foothills. There was always a revival in the Spring after planting, and in the Fall after the harvest was brought in. They were one of the chief social outlets for small, rural communities in the South before mobility and television changed everything. Revivals were called "protracted meetings," since they usually lasted two weeks at a time—which never meant a full fourteen days of preaching each evening, since that would have worn everyone out far too much. But it did mean that the host pastor and the visiting evangelist got out to dinner and supper in the homes of the membership each and every day, gorging on fried chicken, country ham, and homemade biscuits, as if gluttony was not a deadly sin—at least for a preacher!

Miss Minnie Ruth was what folks in church circles called a "big catch." When she professed faith in "the other church," and left the faith of her Deacon father behind, Deacon Stanley

117

was not only humiliated in the community, but his post as Head Deacon at the Baptist Church was also undercut. The old Deacon threw Miss Minnie out of the house in a rage for a few hours, but everyone knew he wouldn't be able to make something so harsh stick for very long. Of course, he let her come back home, and then woefully trudged down the road to the Baptist Church to resign his office in shame. When he handed over his letter of resignation to the Church Clerk, a formidable woman who also happened to be the head of the Women's Missionary Union, she refused it.

"But what else am I to do, Sister?" he protested to her. "I can't be Head Deacon up here any longer. Why, I can't even rule my own household, and control my own teenage daughter!"

The WMU President said, "Deac, you've got a quilting frame up in your attic, don't ye?"

"Why, yes, the Missus, does. How come?"

"You just have your wife set it up and have it ready for the Sisterhood on Saturday morning, hear? And make sure Minnie is home. We're gonna have us a quilting party!"

So, Deacon Stanley did as told. On Saturday morning, the sisters from the Women's Missionary Union showed up on cue at the Stanley home, and swept young Minnie upstairs with them to quilt the day away. The Baptist women strategically bookended her between them against the far wall, hemming her in between their ample bodies so that she could not escape—and the quilting party became a "Quilt and Quote" Inquisition, organized just for the wayward daughter.

The WMU women had rehearsed their arguments all week, so they believed they were more than ready for young Minnie Ruth. They'd quilt a while, and quote a while; quilt a while, and quote a while! Point by point, the women took apart every substantial or imagined idea favorable to the Campbellite religion, taking pains to underline that defection to such a group was far worse than "John Barleycorn, nicotine, and the evils of these." So, when they believed they had done the best job they could answering and exploding every erroneous idea Miss Minnie could possible have in her hard head, the President of the WMU stuck her needle into the cotton batting, turned to her quarry, crossed her arms over her bosoms, and said rather smugly:

"Now, Minnie, that you've heard all of this here, how do ye feel about yerself?"

Miss Minnie took her time, holding her tongue until the anticipation near 'bout ruined them all, and finally spoke:

"Well, I feel like this. I feel just like a grain of wheat . . . in a box full of *rat turds!*"

With a satisfied smile, Irene noted that Miss Minnie had held down her pew at Salem Fork Church for the last sixty years.

Irene's house sat below a cow pasture that bordered the Salem Fork Church cemetery. Beyond the cemetery stood the brick veneer church building, topped with a modest steeple. Whenever the bell rang for Sunday School and Church, Irene heard it first. Many's the year, season in and season out, that she must have gazed up beyond the cows and the grave stones toward the greatest sign of hope in her life.

She sang bass in the church choir. That's right, bass. And, according to our Cousin Doris, the church pianist, Irene had "perfect pitch." She could always be counted on to hit the opening note of an anthem or hymn exactly, setting the rest of the choir on tune firmly, like a coal train on a trestle. Irene was the anchor for the choir, and a pillar of the Church who could dependably pray in public at the drop of a hat, whenever called upon by the Preacher or the Superintendent of Sunday School.

But in my heart of hearts, I know she would rather have preached from the pulpit. She was my biggest fan, and my truest supporter in my quest to "make a preacher." I suppose she wanted me to know the fulfillments of a vocation she always had, but was never allowed to exercise. Women as preachers were unheard of in those days, at the foot of the Blue Ridge Mountains. In my better moments, when I am less self-absorbed than normal, as I ascend a pulpit, I see the twinkle in her eyes in the treasure house of my memory. And, I give thanks for my Aunt Irene, wise in all things, light of the Campbellites, lover of my soul, and the true First Preacher of our family.

Oh, Sweet Mystery of Life!

Sex. It was the word never spoken in mountain country, but the subject was never far from anyone's mind. If John Milton were born in the Blue Ridge Mountains rather than stodgy Olde England, he might have been remembered for a steamy hillbilly coming of age classic—something like "Innocence Lost." Sex was at the heart of everything in Southern culture, and just because it was never mentioned in "decent" company, that didn't mean any good Southerner wanted to be free of it. Sex was an intricate dance between puritanical religion and moonshine whiskey. The dance steps of mating were kept as hidden as a liquor still from the Revenuers. But, as I grew up, it seemed to me everybody knew that "sex" was the unspoken name for the only dance there is. Why else would the Baptists so vehemently prohibit their kids from dancing, then? Preachers knew (probably from their own experience in the backseat of the car) that dancing was the first slippery slide down the slick slope that ended by creating "The Beast With Two Backs."

No moment in sexual history is as fraught with mystery, dread, and titillation as The First Date (cue the spooky music!). "I'm too shy to ask anybody to go out—what do I do? Oh, Lawdy! What do I do? What if she doesn't like me? What if I fail at being a stud, and turn out to be a dud? Can you get a girl pregnant from kissing!?!"

I couldn't drive a car for my first date. Dad did the driving . . . and the coaching.

Just because the Baptists didn't like dances, they had no way to outlaw them at the Elementary School gymnasium. Anybody remember "Sock Hops"? Shoes were not allowed on the basketball court. Dating couples scooted around in their Bobbie Sox. I got up the courage to ask the cutest, prettiest, most popular girl in the Eighth Grade to go out with me for my First Date, Pamela Gean, and she said "Yes!" Whoo-hoo!

But as the night of the Sock Hop approached, I got cold feet big time! Sure, I had bragged all over school about being a stud duck, since Pamela Gean agreed to be my date. It was fun watching the other guys turn green with envy, wondering how "Ol' Four-Eyes" (I wore glasses) got the hottest girl in school to go out with him. But as the reality of dating a woman with "experience" set in, I started to get performance shy. I had practiced with my cousins doing the Twist and the Mashed Potato, and Susan and Jane assured me that there was nothing to slow dancing—you just held tight and shuffled your feet. But what about kissing? Should you kiss on the First Date? How? Tongues? No tongues? Dry? Wet? Should you ask first, or just go for it, or instead just walk her to the door, shake her hand, and say "Goodnight"?

Hell, it was one thing to practice dancing with your first cousins—but God knows you couldn't practice kissing with anybody!

Dad couldn't have been more perfect that night. He drove me over to Pamela Gean's house and didn't say a word. 'Course, he did sneak a peak at the way I put the fancy orchid corsage I bought for her on her wrist (she seemed so thrilled!). He waited patiently with the other fathers and uncles and brothers outside the gym while all us kids boogied the night away. I remember that the DJ played a tune from my favorite group, "The Lovin' Spoonful": "Did You Ever Have To Make Up Your Mind?/Say Yes To One, And Leave The Other Behind?" Pamela Gean and I could sing the words by heart, right in time with the record. The night was going great!

On the way home, however, my nerves began to get the better of me. As I sat on my side of the backseat and Pam sat on hers, I fretted over how to conclude the night. Dad seemed to be suffering from a rare sort of tic in his neck and head. Poor guy! He kept looking at me in the rearview mirror of the Roadmaster, jerking his head toward the passenger side door, over and over. I didn't catch on to what he was trying to get me to do until we had already turned up Pam's parents' driveway.

To kiss, or not to kiss, that was the question making my heart pound in my chest as I played the gentleman, got out of my side of the car, and walked over to open her door. She walked on just a bit ahead of me toward the porch, where the light was shining in anticipation of her return from the big date. I had just begun what felt like a gallows walk behind her, when Dad rolled down his car window, and spoke the first words to me all night.

"Pssst! Pssst! Hey, Boy, come over here!" he said in a stage whisper. "Boy, listen to your Ol' Daddy! This is the only First Date you'll ever have, so here is what you do: Get up there with her on that porch, jump on her back, pinch her tail and make her squeal! Hear what I'm telling ye?"

"Huh?" I said.

"I said, 'Go up there, jump-on-her-back-and-pinch-her-tail-and-make-her-squeal!' Ain't you got no gumption?"

In retrospect, Dad was speaking with me metaphorically. All he wanted to get me to do was kiss her. Being a youth in fundamentalist country, however, I took him literally. Pamela Gean sure threw a mean haymaker (and she should have)! I came back to the car with a black eye. But before she stepped into the house, Pam dropped her guard just an instant, and I could've sworn I saw the edges of her lips curl up in a wicked little smile—at my expense.

(Cue the French horns from the score of Young Frankenstein): "Oh, Sweet Mystery of Life, At La-a-a-a-st I Found You . . . !"

Bubblegum Blackmail

It is a wonder that any of us ever got an education in high school! Too many she-nanigans went on to learn much. My freshman class resembled the Island of Broken Toys : Frances the Mule (Hee-Haw!), Fat Man, Barny Be-Damned, Big Red, Curious George, Eek-us a-Freak-us, and Flush!

We had nicknames for all our poor teachers, too: Flounder Foot, our female calculus teacher who clomped along in size-12s; Roho, the principle; Mr. Bat-shit, the social studies teacher; Lurch, the over-tall civics teacher; Prissy Boy, the music instructor; and Maggot-mouth (damn, we were cruel!), the algebra teacher, Prissy Boy's girlfriend. Then there was the new French and Speech and Comp Teacher, Ms. Manners!

Ms. Manners resembled one of the prancing hippopatomi (or is it, "hippopatomuses"?) that danced the "Waltz of the Flowers" in tutus and ballet toe shoes in Walt Disney's Fantasia. She tippie-toed everywhere, and her favorite expression was, "Shush! You have a demerit!" She virtually populated the study hall Mr. Bat-shit ran after school with students she sent into detention. Not that we didn't deserve it, mind you.

Never register for Elementary French for first period. 8 a.m. is too early for God to get up, not to mention for French. *"Repeter, s'il vous plait,"* first thing in the morning . . . *mon dieu!*

Barney Be-damned was the ringleader of our discontent. He was gobby-fat, with a Moe-from-the-Three-Stooges hair cut, and pimples pinking his big, floppy jowls. Curious George was his toady. Barney's whole purpose in first period was to torment Ms. Manners, and drive her out of teaching into something like . . . long haul trucking, maybe.

Barney would smuggle a straight pin from home, and perforate the illustrations in the French textbook we had, *Écouter et Lirer* (Listen and Read, for the un-Gallicized). Perforation was a morning ritual of his.

"Pop-puh-pop-pop!" "Here, have an Eiffel Tower!" and Barney Be-damned would pop a picture la tour Eiffel right off the page.

"Pop-puh-pop-pop!" "Here, have an Arc of Triumph!" "Pop-puh-pop-pop!" "Here, have a *jeune fille!*" "Pop-puh-pop-pop-pop!"

Barney turned his textbook into confetti.

One morning, Barney came to class with a dollar's worth of Bazooka bubble gum in his jowl. A dollar's worth of bubble gum is a lot even now, and back in the day, it was much more than that! He could bite down on a bubble, and make it crack like a cap pistol! "Ker-pow!!" On the morning in question, Ms. Manners heard at least one snap and pop too many for her.

"Barney, get that mass of disgusting pink material out of your mouth this instant!" she demanded.

"Right-O, Mama Bear!" he said (don't ask me why; he just called her that). With one deft move, he pried the bubble gum out of his jaw, and dumped it right in the middle of *Écouter et Lirer*. He slapped the covers shut, and turned the book into a sticky pink accordion.

"Eeek! You've turned that book into trash, young man! I guess you know you've bought that book now, don't you?"

"Right-O, Mama Bear!" he said. Out came the straight pin. "Pop-puh-pop-pop!" "Here, have yourself a Notre Dame, then!"

Probably the most irritated Ms. Manners ever got with Barney Be-damned was the day he decided to mock everything she said by feigning astonishment, and saying, "Re-mark-able!" after every sentence she spoke (something he'd picked up from watching reruns of The Little Rascals on TV.)

She: "We have a test on Friday, class!"

He: "Re-mark-able!"

She: "So study your verbs."

He: "Re-mark-able!"

She: "Barney! You better watch it!"

He: "Re-mark-able!"

She: "If you say that one more time, you're going to detention! I swear it!"

He: "Fan-tas-tic!" He simply changed word after word after each time Ms. Manners threatened him with detention: "Stu-pen-dous!" "Un-be-lieve-able!" et cetera, et cetera.

Finally, in sheer exasperation, Ms. Manners tippie-toed over to him and said: "Barney, see my teacher's version of the textbook? It has all the answers in it. See how heavy and thick it is? If you dare to say ONE MORE WORD, I am going to HIT you over the head with this book, you hear me?"

He, as snidely as he could: *"Apple-sauce!"*

And the French textbook, teacher's edition, with all the answers in it, fell from on high right on top of Barney's head like a Steinway piano in a cartoon! "TH-Whack!" It made his teeth pop! No matter if he was expecting it, the force of the whack took him by surprise—you could tell by his bulging eyes!

"See, I told you," she said, as she tippie-toed away with a little giggle.

We knew right then and there that trouble was coming. Barney Be-damned looked like he had a thundercloud gathering on top of his head!

"You won't know when it's coming, Mama Bear!" he hissed. "But I'll get you if it's the last thing I ever do, and I mean good!"

We weren't expecting retribution so soon, or on such a scale. The very next day in class, Barney showed up early, something he never did for first period. He had three cans of butane lighter fluid, the kind used for cigarette lighters. Frances the Mule, Big Red, and I watched in disbelief as he patiently crawled around the classroom, applying the lighter fluid to the baseboard of the walls ("pokketta, pokketta, pokketta!"). He used up two cans on the baseboards, and squirted a whole can down the screw holes in the aluminum threshold across the bottom of the door to the hall.

Barney sent his henchman, Curious George, to scout for Mama Bear. "Tell me when the Bear steps over the threshold, Curious!" not bothering to disguise the venom in his voice. And then Barney hid behind a bookcase, whipped out and flipped open his Zippo lighter so it was lit.

Momentarily, here came Ms. Manners, chugging along with books and papers up to her rather ample chin, as usual. She tippie-toed with one foot over the threshold, and in mid-stride, Curious George yelled, "NOW!"

Barney touched fire to the butane lighter fluid on the baseboard, and blue flame raced around the room from both the left and the right, streaking toward the booby-trapped aluminum threshold. "Whoosh! Whoosh! Whoosh!" the fire went, and then it hit the threshold:

"KA-POW-EEE!!!"

Blue fire lept up half way to the ceiling! Ms. Manners threw the books and papers in all directions! We fell in the floor, laughing and gasping for air from astonishment!

Barney jumped out from his hiding place, yelling at the top of his voice:

"Indian attack! Indian attack! Get your wagons in a circle! They'll scalp you! Women and children first! Women and children first! Indian attack!"

We shrieked with laughter!

Ms. Manners, regardless of her bulk, moved like greased lightning, grabbing Barney two-handed by the jowls! She was singed medium rare but otherwise unhurt. Her mascara ran in streaks down her cheeks, her hair looked like a coon dog had run through it, and she had a look on her face like the Grim Reaper at a train wreck!

Shaking him by the jowls, she shouted in staccato, "I-AM-GOING-TO-SEE-THAT-YOU-GO-TO-THE-STATE-PENITENTIARY-FOR-THIS, DO YOU HEAR ME!! I-AM-GOING-TO-SEE-TO-IT-PERSONALLY-THAT-YOU-WILL-NEVER-BE-IN-ANOTHER-CLASSROOM-IN-NORTH-CAROLINA!! AAARRRGHH!!"

Cool as a sniper drawing down on his target, Barney said in a level voice, "You do that, Mama Bear, and I'll tell everything I know about you and Sandy Belo down on the riverbank!"

Looking at him with horror, she abruptly turned him loose, and then hightailed it to the teacher's restroom to regroup. She just let him go! Nothing so far as any of us knew was ever said about what had happened that morning, and, apparently, nobody in Principal Roho's office was ever any the wiser. Barney had somehow caught Ms. Manners shacking up with a man down on Fisher's River. No school board in North Carolina would continue to employ a teacher who fornicated, back in those days.

It was blackmail, pure and simple—with the scent of bubblegum, toasted panty hose, and butane lighter fluid hovering around it.

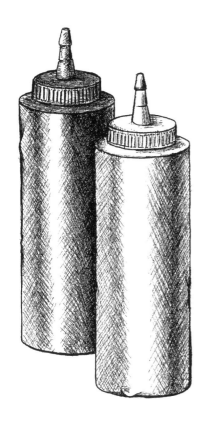

Career Woman

Aunt Lora's apartment in Greensboro was one of the few places Mama and Daddy allowed me to go for overnight visits—sometimes even for a few days! Lora was what people in the '50s and '60s called a "career woman." That meant she was a self-sufficient woman who lived for her job and never married a man.

She and her friend Ruth lived in an upstairs apartment. They had a framed Saturday Evening Post magazine cover of President John F. Kennedy on the dining room wall, the famous one by Norman Rockwell. JFK's eyes in that portrait freaked me out. They seemed to follow me wherever I went. Sometimes, even when I sat with my back to him, it felt like President Kennedy was looking at me. Creepy! I hung a paper towel over the picture so I wouldn't be so self-conscious in Lora's house.

Lora was a truly independent woman. She smoked Pall Malls. She never dated. She was the first female I ever knew who flew on airplanes. I took my first plane trip with her. Before we boarded the jet (nobody "pre-boarded" in those days, thank God!), she insisted that I fill out an airline insurance policy, available from machines near the gate, and name her the beneficiary. "If we crash, and I live, at least something good will come out of it," she said—hardly a comfort to me.

Funny—Lora sort of relished getting crank calls on her bedside telephone. Nothing kinky, I believe. At least I never caught wind of any type of prurient interest on her part. She just enjoyed the verbal jiu jitsu. Come to think of it, she actually listed her name and marital status in the phone book: "Miss Lora Martin." Kinda daring the creepers to call, no? The nasty-minded did call sometimes, the kind who breathed heavily and asked which one of the two "girls" who lived there was "the man." Lora had a put down ready to go for most any situation.

One night very late, the phone rang her awake from a deep slumber, and she answered it in her deep alto voice, made all the deeper by years of smoking, "H-e-l-l-o."

Nasty Man on the other end of the line: "Is this Hell? Let me speak to the Devil!"

Without missing a beat, Lora replied, "Speaking!" Her would-be prankster, dumbfounded, just hung up.

I loved to go with Lora to work. She was the receptionist and bookkeeper for Mother Murphy's Laboratories, a firm owned and operated by two brothers, Mr. Pete Murphy, and Mr. Kermit Murphy. Mother Murphy's manufactured flavoring for confectioners and bakers all along the East Coast. Huge stainless steel kettles, stories high, dominated the warehouse where the flavorings, especially several varieties of vanilla flavoring, were brewed. The whole place smelled like a big vanilla bean, and the scent lingered in Lora's clothes long after she left from work.

Mr. Dobbins, the chemist, was a favorite of mine. He wore a white lab coat, and dabbled around his test tubes and extract bottles day-in-and-day-out. He looked like a kindly Dr. Frankenstein in his half-specs, using the candy flavorings, I suspected, for a clever cover up as he secretly concocted something taboo and verboten. I expected one day to hear him in his lab laughing maniacally and shouting, "It's Alive! It's Alive! Bwahahaha!" His big joke was to get a sucker to sniff a couple of nice vanilla extract samples, and then slip in something particularly noxious that he called "goat extract," with a punch as strong as smelling salts. "Oops!" he'd lie, "Forgot that one was in here."

I owe Lora a lot. She never underestimated me, as adults often do to children. She opened new worlds to me, whole new worlds that one day would launch me into forms of advocacy I had never dreamed of as a boy. One afternoon in the early Spring of 1960, as I finished playing around her desk, she told me we were going downtown right after work because there was something she wanted me to see. I was so excited! Mr. Pete, the brother who looked like Boris Karloff to me, stepped out of his office and asked, "Miss Martin, where are you and Little Stevie (Ugh! "Little Stevie" made my skin crawl!) going this evening?"

"We're going down to the Courthouse, Mr. Murphy," she said.

"Miss Martin!" he exclaimed, "surely you are not going to take a child down there, are you? Why, it isn't safe!"

"Yes, Mr. Murphy, I most certainly am," she replied so resolutely he dared not question further. "This is history, and I intend for him to be part of it."

He shook his head, and retreated to his office while we bustled out the door to Lora's car.

The largest crowd of people I had ever seen were crowded around the Guilford County Courthouse lawn, surrounding what seemed to be an ocean of black people sitting arm-in-arm on the grass. I was eight, going on nine, but small for my age, so Lora gripped my hand firmly as she angled through the crowd to the curb surrounding the lawn—a front row view for her nephew.

All around us were loud, pushy white people, people who seemed agitated and angry at the black people seated on the yard. Earlier that year, a group of young black university students had started the first sit-in protest in the nation at the F.W. Woolworth lunch counter in downtown Greensboro, and the non-violent movement for civil rights had spread like wildfire. The sit-ins had gotten so large that this one occupied the whole Courthouse lawn. Lora had chosen her side. She might be from redneck Surry County, as segregated as any place in the Tarheel State, but her sympathies lay with the black folk blanketing the lawn.

Apart from a few cops who seemed to look the other way, the rest of the surrounding mob of white people scared me. I gripped Lora's hand tighter, as men around us hurled epithets like brickbats at the peaceful black people seated, singing, "I Ain't Gonna Let Nobody Turn Me 'Round." I could see Confederate flags sprout up from the mob, and I heard loud music blaring from bullhorns that I learned later were broadcasting "Reb-Time" songs like "Move Them N****rs North" by Col. Sharecropper. Girls screamed and shrieked, and redneck young men balled up their fists and shook them at the protestors.

A big, elderly white woman right next to me who wore a short sleeve blouse was particularly agitated. She bared her teeth, revealing that two were missing, and flapped her arms wildly in the air. A fat woman still, she had lost enough weight to turn the flesh of her arms into enormous flaps of loose skin, wings of meat that flogged the air as she flailed her arms and shook her fists. She yelled, over and over, "N****r! N****r! Don't yew *wish* yew was white! Don't yew *wish* yew was white!" I could see the tendons straining in her neck as she raged on and on.

Somebody had unlocked a café on the Courthouse Square, and distributed red and yellow plastic squirt bottles of ketch-up and mustard to a crew of young white bucks who broke the flimsy police line with no resistance, and spread out among the seated black folk. Laughing like lunatics, the white men squirted great splashes of ketchup and mustard in the ears, all over the hair, and up the noses of the non-violent protes-tors, humiliating them and trying their best to provoke a fight for the local television cameras. But the black folk endured everything, and kept on singing, arm-in-arm: "Ain't gonna let se-gre-ga-tion turn me 'round/I'm gonna keep on a'walkin,' keep on a'talking, marchin' up to Freedom Land!"

Something happened to me that day. I changed in ways I couldn't yet understand. The two of us stood there, quiet in a boiling sea of anger made up of people who looked like us—facing a panorama of dignified people who looked so very different from us.

I looked up at my Aunt Lora whose gaze was fixed on the scene before us. A tear slowly rolled down her cheek. I squeezed her hand. She squeezed back.

She was right . . . it sure enough was History that unfolded before our eyes that day. The lesson she taught me by braving her fears and the fears of her boss set me on a path I am still "a'walkin,'"—long after she has gone.

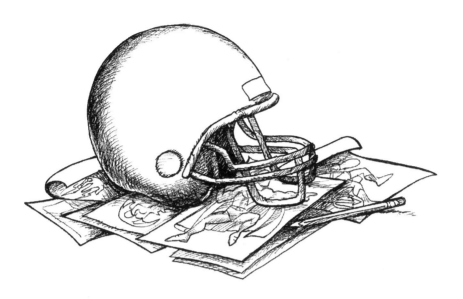

Big Two-Tootie-Two

"Beef" was my best friend in school. He earned his nick-name because he was strong as a bull. We bonded because we both loved art and football. Our families knew each other from 'way 'way back. Matter of fact, further back than I had any way of knowing, as I learned from Beef's tiny little grand-mother. One of the first times I went home from school with him, his grandmother met us on the sidewalk, took one look at me, and hollered out:

"Lord, have mercy! You're Hazel and Thed's young un! I can see the favor! C'mon over here, child! I knowed you 'fore you was even BORN!" (I'm still trying to figure that one out. She squeezed on me till my eyes bugged out.)

The time I spent at Beef's house was magical. He could

draw anything with a pencil. And he was fast, too! Crowd scenes were Beef's specialty, and he loved to draw Super Heroes: Thing, and Cat Woman, and Wolverine—Superman, Captain America, and the Silver Surfer! Why, he could draw a human hand and make it look so lifelike (which I believe is the hardest part of the human form for an artist to master)! He made me green with envy. Beef introduced me to Jimi Hendrix, too. His bedroom walls were covered with Hendrix posters, and Beef had the first black light I had ever seen, which was the coolest thing, ever ("You were expecting me to have a *white* light, were you?" he would tease). We would switch off the overhead light, turn on the black light, and listen to "Purple Haze" over and over. Beef and I weren't stoners. I didn't even smoke cigarettes—but I could've sworn Hendrix was singing about Man Love in that first stanza:

"S'cooze me while I kiss this guy!"

I was always welcome at Beef's house, even though his mother was struggling with lupus, the disease that eventually took her life. But Beef was not welcome at mine. My stepmother refused to let him sit at our dining room table. Dad tried to smooth things over, but the damage was already done, as far as I was concerned. That was the only time I ever ran away from home, because my friend was not welcome there. I left for three days, staying with other friends I could swear to secrecy. Dad was wild with worry, which made me sorry about what I had done. But I was angry and heart broken. I came back home, but things were never quite the same with my stepmother. She wasn't a mean person, actually. She was great for my Dad, filling a hole in his heart after my mother died so untimely. But my stepmother was blind on this subject, so fearful that she would shake and tremble when the prospect of a black person eating at her dinner table came up. Beef, to his great credit, never held it against her, or my dad. The biggest thing I learned out of that troubled time is how difficult it is to blend families.

Friendship must be the strongest thing in the world. Not only did my friendship with Beef survive the incident at my house—it grew as we entered high school together, Class of '70.

I loved sports, but as a spectator, not a player. Beef, on the other hand, excelled at football. He lifted weights and ran track. And he got BIG! Monster size! As a linebacker on the junior varsity team, Beef dressed out at 222 lbs. That won him his other nickname, the one they gave him on the squad: "Big Two-Tootie-Two." By the time he made the varsity team, Beef had the power of a runaway locomotive.

I became a sports writer for the Elkin (NC) Tribune, and, because I had the gift of gab, a play-by-play broadcast announcer for home games:

"Good evening, La-dies and Gen-tle-men! And welcome to football at its finest, tonight between the Surry Central Golden Eagles and the Forbush Falcons! Tonight's broadcast from Golden Eagle Field on WPAQ-Radio is sponsored by The Discount House, downtown Mount Airy on Willow Street, and the Dowell Brothers Cost-Plus Supermarket, Highway 52 South of Mount Airy! This week's Dowell Boys Special is T-Bone steak, fresh off the hoof! And, remember, you can't beat the Dowell Boys meat (I didn't write 'em, I just read 'em the way my radio boss wrote 'em)!"

In the background, over the roar of the crowd, you could

hear the Central Cheerleaders singing their hearts out:

"Oh, when those Gol-den Ea-gles fall in line/they're
gonna win the game for sure this time!
And for the dear old team we love so well/we're gonna
join to-geth-er and you'll hear us yell!
For Surry Central's Ea-gles can't be beat/we send the
other team back in defeat!
And, so, when this game's done, we'll win another one/
SCHS! SCHS! (Rah! Rah! Rah!) SCHS!"

I learned the broadcast trade from Ol' Man Ceece Bennett, WPAQ's septuagenarian announcer, who wrote up all the copy we used on football nights.

His countrified double entendre was scandalous! That's why he was so popular with the redneck crowd along the Blue Ridge. His gravely, sing-songy voice and nasal twang were everywhere on the radio:

"Y'all come on down to the Discount House, downtown Mount Airy on-a Will-er Street! All you movie stars, we got sunglasses at the Discount House! And all you women! Now hear this! We got a new shipment of panties! We got a big sale on women's panties, half-off and still droppin'!"

Beef and I graduated from Surry Central High. We went our separate ways to college, and beyond. I hear he made it big, and moved down to Raleigh, the state capital. Seems only yesterday that I saw him charging down the field, dressed in a uniform of gold-and-black-and-white, head down and scattering Forbush Falcons right and left, sacking the quarterback! Big Two-Tootie-Two, my friend, *"fore I'se ever born!"*

GORGOSAURUS

Al Capone, Allosaurus, and Me

Lost and Found. Déjà vu. Searching for the Lost Ark. Everybody is looking for something to recapture: a moment, a memory, the feeling of a hand in ours. Me, too.

I keep going back to Chicago, the Windy City, to find mine.

Traveling to Chicago on the train was the most exciting trip of my youth. I was eight. Can you imagine how spectacular, how overwhelming the Big City was to a little hillbilly boy who had been beyond the borders of North Carolina perhaps once in his life? Mama organized the whole adventure for us—my Aunt Lora, my cousin Whitey (Aunt Irene's boy), and me. We met our Michigan relatives, my Aunt Joyce, my Uncle Art, and my cousins Susan and Jane, at the grandiose

143

Pick Congress Hotel, right on Michigan Avenue in the South Loop. That visit to the Windy City, unknown to any of us at the time, was the last vacation my mother would ever take with us again. Perhaps the combination of the wonder of my first encounter with a mega-city, and the aching memories of being so supremely happy with Mama there has made Chicago far more than just another destination throughout my lifetime. It has become the Jerusalem of my memories, the Bethlehem to which I repeatedly return to reclaim the warmth of her hand in mine. Chicago, you see, is my chosen Pilgrim's Rest. But my pilgrim journeys there never seem to become a resting place.

Oh, the wonder and joy of that first Chicagoland expedition! We boarded the train in Asheville, snaking our way over the backbone of the Great Smokey Mountains and then across the midriff of the nation to Chi-Town. My first cousin Whitey (aka Phil) was the perfect companion. He was slightly older, an only child just like me. The train was better than a Disneyland ride for two small boys who never had such an experience before. Mama booked us a Pullman compartment all our own. The fixtures were perfectly boy sized, and dropped right out of the walls, to our giddy delight: the little lavatory, the tiny toilet, and the cozy little shower, all replete with knobs and handles, and hot and cold running water! Where in the world does all that hot water come from, we wondered? Would somebody please explain the endless fascination boys have with toilet bowls and bodily functions?

We both had to break the bowl in as soon as we could, just so we could hear the gadget flush.

At bedtime, the porter knocked on our door, pulled down the sleeping compartments for Whitey and me, and spread the covers for us. Each night on the train, we fell asleep, lullabied by the rhythm of steel wheels rumbling over the rails, the clickety-clack of a mighty train drawing us northward through the night.

Breakfast was served on linen and china in the meal car. We were ravenous by the time for our family reservation. Our eggs and bacon vanished so quickly they were barely tasted, and Whitey and I took off exploring. Mama and Lora relaxed, knowing that up and down the train cars was as far as we could go. They got a second cup of coffee, and retired to the observation deck to watch the Midwest go by.

To Whitey and me, every bend in the rail lines was a hideout for outlaws or bands of wild Indians who would ambush our train, just like in the movies . . . or on Tweetsie! The Tweetsie Railroad was the only experience Whitey and I had with train travel prior to the Chicago trip. Our parents had taken us to ride the narrow gauge rail line that once served the mountains of North Carolina from Boone to Blowing Rock commercially, but then became a tourist attraction after being made obsolete by more powerful freight trains and big rig trucks.

Tweetsie was a coal fired, steam powered locomotive that pulled its wooden and steel carriages from its original depot through the new Wild West Town and around a three mile loop—its steam whistle screaming through the hills and hollows. On my visit to Tweetsie, I was ready for anything. I had my official Davy Crockett coonskin cap on my head, my toy Kentucky long rifle slung over my arm, and my rubber-bladed tomahawk tucked in my belt. Another little boy turned up his nose at my get-up. He sported a bright red Roy Rogers cowboy hat, red cowboy boots, and a couple of fake pearl-handled cap pistols buckled over a set of fringed western chaps. "Roy" drew those six shooters and peeled his eyes out the train window, ready to mete out frontier justice to train robbers, renegades, and other bad actors. Imagine our surprise when war painted Indians charged into the rear of our rail car, howling at the top of their lungs! "Roy Rogers" couldn't draw down on anything—he froze and dropped both his pistols on the floor (I didn't do much better!)! With an ear-splitting whoop, the chief of the war party picked up "Roy's" red cowboy hat and ran his fingers through his hair—then bounded off of the moving train with his braves in tow, leaving his little quarry crying for his mother because he had lost control of his bowels, and filled his britches but good! "Roy's" mother beseeched the conductor to stop the train just long enough for her to take her son down to the nearest creek and wash out his drawers. I sat back in my seat self-satisfied as "Roy"-with-the-dripping-drawers and his mama reboarded. I hugged my trusty rifle and hummed, "Da-vee, Davy Crockett, King of the Wild Frontier!"

Our headquarters in Chi-Town was the Congress Hotel, the largest place I had ever seen—over 700 rooms! The Congress had the reputation of being "Chicago's Most Haunted Hotel," to the endless glee of my three first cousins and me. "Scarface" Al Capone, the gangster boss of bosses, and a notorious member of his gang, Jake "Greasy Thumb" Guzik, had lived there, and some on the staff said they had seen Capone's ghost roaming the corridors, still breathing out threats after all these years. Once in a blue moon, the ghost of a murdered homeless man, Peg Leg Johnny, could be heard stumping along the halls of the Congress. And then there was Room 441. Hotel security is called up to 441 more than any other room. Spooked-out guests report objects moving around with no apparent cause, weird sounds, and the ghostly outline of a woman moving through the walls! We kids dashed back and forth past the door just to see if ol' Scarface himself would jump out and grab us!

 Those days were full of Chicago magic! We visited the Museum of Science and Industry to walk through the giant human heart, strolled along the Lakefront, and toured the Shedd Aquarium, Chicago's Inland Sea. But for me, the deepest impressions on my young soul were left by the visit to the Field Museum. You see, I am forever a dinosaur geek at heart. The first intellectual blossoming of my tiny mind was learning how to spell the names of the prehistoric monsters that populated my dreams—"T-y-r-a-n-n-o-s-a-u-r-u-s R-e-x" ("King Tyrant Lizard"); "T-r-i-c-e-r-a-t-o-p-s" ("Three-horned Face"); and "B-r-o-n-t-o-s-a-u-r-u-s" ("Thunder Lizard"). That had earned me my Dobson School nickname, "Dinosaurus Sprink." Had life taken a different turn for me, rather than becoming a theologian and minister, I would surely have become a paleontologist, reveling in the bones of beasts long turned to stone. I enjoy the life that chose me—don't get me wrong about that! Still, I often wonder if I would not be happier today if I had taken the dusty trail that led to the dinosaur hunting grounds.

Before walking through the massive doors of the Field Museum, I had never personally witnessed the fossil of any Terrible Lizard. There, in the Great Hall, towering over me, stood a nightmare from the dawn of time! My mouth went dry! "Allosaurus!" I whispered out with a rasp. The great meat eater with its immense jaws full of steak knife teeth stood fully erect, looming over its prey, the remains of a duck-billed had-rosaur. Like a hungry assassin, the sightless orbits in its pre-historic killer's skull seemed to consider me for dessert, and its little two-fingered claws seemed to clutch and release in time with my heartbeat.

Oh, there were lots of things wrong with that picture, mistakes of a small boy who thought he knew more than he did, but also the mistakes of paleontologists whose under-standing of dinosaurs has undergone a sea change since that day in 1961. For one thing, the posture of the mounted fos-sils was all wrong in those days. The Terrible Lizard I saw in the Great Hall was posed like a gargantuan kangaroo—body erect upon straight legs like tree trunks, with a tail dragging the ground behind. That was the best science could do in the early days of John F. Kennedy's presidency. Dinos were thought to be cold-blooded, slow moving and dim witted, like iguanas in molasses, many of them relying on swamp water to displace the burden of so much body weight. Don't blame the paleontologists—everybody believed it. Now, thanks to generations of dinosaur heretics who proposed new theories and supported them by painstaking research, we know that dinosaurs were very likely warm-blooded, social (especially the pack hunters like the mighty meat eaters of the Jurassic and the Cretaceous), and some as swift-footed as race horses. Museum mounts reflect the change, too. Today, fossil displays are shown swept forward with mighty tails held straight out from the hips for balance and swift turning capability, menac-ing the modern day viewer with the prospect of breathtaking speed and pursuit intelligence.

I had completely misidentified my monster that day, too. The species before me was not Allosaurus, the apex predator of the Jurassic, but Gorgosaurus, the "Gorgon Lizard," a T. Rex cousin from the Cretaceous. None of that mattered to me on that summer day in the Great Hall. I stood transfixed before the first fossil meat-o-saur I had ever seen. One thing did ring true about this beast, however, even as I misnamed it and missed its time in the sun by 70 million years or so. "Gorgosaurus" was named for the three Gorgons, mythical monster sisters with snakes for hair whose gaze turned their victims to stone. That was pretty much what it felt like to me, gawping upward with my little mouth open. I couldn't move. Never mind. Mama was right there at my side. No harm comes to children whose mothers are standing there beside them, right?

I guess I could be forgiven for mistakenly identifying that ancient predator as an Allosaur. The first meat eating dinosaur ever to make its debut in the movies was an Allosaurus in *The Lost World*, circa 1925. It was only after King Kong in 1933 that Tyrannosaurus overshadowed Allosaurus as the most fearsome dino of filmland. Whitey and I had seen the 1956 cowboys-and-dinosaurs movie at the Dobson Drive-In, *The Beast of Hollow Mountain*, starring manly Guy Madison as the roping cowhand Jimmy Ryan, sultry Patricia Medina as *femme fatale* Sarita, and child actor Mario Navarro as the boy Panchito. The stop-action Allosaur, however, was the real star of the show. The plot was pretty tiresome. An American cowboy living in Mexico discovers that a prehistoric monster is eating his cattle. After a series of stock sequence close calls, Cowboy Jimmy rescues the beautiful Sarita and the hapless little Panchito from certain death in the jaws of the Hollow Mountain monster, and lures the beast into quicksand. *Finis.* Fade to black, as Cowboy Jimmy and Sarita embrace, and are then nearly tackled by a big squeeze from Panchito, suitably grateful not to have become a monster's first hors d'oeuvre of the evening. Did I see my Mama in Sarita, and myself in little Panchito with the sombrero? Who knows? But the Allosaurus special effects in *The Beast of Hollow Mountain* were pretty damned convincing, and became an archetype in my boyish mind.

That trip Mama planned was so successful, she told her sisters that she intended to make a train trip an annual affair for her nieces, her nephew, and me. The very next year, she said, we were going south of the border, to Mexico! But cancer intervened. Our Chicago trip was the last one she ever made.

There are moments that define and haunt us, aren't there? Lost and Found. Déjà vu. The Search for the Lost Ark. I go back to Chicago from time to time, and when I do, I always try to take the train, at least part of the way there. It only seems right to do it that way. Every time, I make my way back to the Great Hall of the Field Museum. These days the Gorgosaurus is long gone. Its spectacular replacement is the Rock Star of the dino world, Tyrannosaurus Sue—the largest, most complete skeleton of a tyrannosaur in existence. The Field Museum has done a great job with her. Flocks of children and their parents crowd the rails bordering her display, snapping photos in the shadow of her jaws. She strides across the Cretaceous wilderness like a predatory nightmare, afraid of nothing, the Mistress of her destiny, unaware of the swift coming of the asteroid that will exterminate her kind and change her world forever.

Every time I stand there facing the haunting bones, I find myself inadvertently—unbidden, it seems—reaching slightly upward into the thin air beside me, just a bit to the right . . . searching for Mama's hand.

Epilogue

Honeysuckers live sweet and large. They live as interestingly as your Granny eating an okra sandwich. As a parting gift from one Honeysucker to another, here are a few aphorisms to live by, compliments of Thedford Guy Sprinkle, my Daddy:

- "Never trust a man or a mule that's able to look through the same hole with both eyes. Such a person is too finely bred."

- "Remember: The rat that eats the most fat meat will have the slickest hole" (Me: "Which hole, Daddy?" He: "The rat hole, son!").

- "A man who'll lie will have other bad habits."

- "A mean person is worse than a blue-nosed, stripe-ed-assed snake" (He to Me: "And, Boy, I'm a-telling ye, a stripe-ed-assed snake is the meanest kind of snake!").

- "If a mule kicks you the first time, it's the mule's fault. But if you don't move and the same mule kicks you the second time, it's your own damned fault! Ain't you got no gumption?"

. . . And until we meet again, this little gem Dad offered me on the day he died:

- "Don't worry about anything, Honey. Don't worry about anything at all. And, don't forget to smell the flowers, y'hear?"

A Parting Shot!

Be on the lookout for Volume Two of Honeysucker:
Honeysucker 2:
When East Meets West

More of your favorite High Country humor is on the way!
See y'all again soon, y'hear?

14403508R00089

Made in the USA
San Bernardino, CA
26 August 2014